100 YEARS OF
GRAND PRIX

Celebrating a Century of Grand Prix Racing 1906–2006

First published in 2006 by Touchstone Books Ltd

Touchstone Books Ltd
Highlands Lodge
Chartway Street
Sutton Valence
Kent ME17 3HZ
United Kingdom

www.touchstone-books.com

A copy of the CIP data for this book is available from the British Library upon request.

The rights of Trevor Legate to be identified as the author of this work have been asserted in accordance with Section 77 of the Copyright, Designs and Patents Act of 1988.

Designed by Paul Turner and Sue Pressley
Editorial consultant: Nick Wigley

Printed and bound in Singapore

The author and publishers have made every reasonable effort to contact all copyright holders. Any errors that may have occurred are inadvertent and anyone who for any reason has not been contacted is invited to write to the publishers so that a full acknowledgement may be made in subsequent editions of this work. The opinions expressed in this book are those of the author and not necessarily those of the publishers or their agents.

ISBN: 0-9551020-1-4

Touchstone Books Ltd – A winning combination
Inspired by creativity, driven by enthusiasm, and fuelled by passion!

The team: Trevor Legate is a talented professional photographer, motoring enthusiast, and respected author. As professional graphic designers Paul Turner and Sue Pressley have a long-established reputation for expertise in creating innovative and beautiful books. With 20 years experience in the world of corporate communications, Nick Wigley, a successful historic race car driver, brings creative thinking and entrepreneurial flair to the mix.

Page 1: Many talented drivers have thrilled fans of of motor racing over the past one hundred years. One of the very best was the Canadian driver, Gilles Villeneuve.
Page 3: A moment of Grand Prix history as the Renault of Fernando Alonso crosses the finish line at the 2005 Chinese Grand Prix to become the youngest driver to win the World Championship.
Page 4: During 1950, little thought was given to safety matters and spectators were often very close to the action: the BRM P15 MkI of Peter Walker at the Pedralbes street circuit, Barcelona.

Picture credits
Collection Serge Pozzolli: 1, 4, 12, 13, 14, 15, 16 (t), 17, 18, 19, 20, 21, 22, 23, 24, 25, 26, 27, 28, 29, 30, 31, 32, 33, 34/35, 36, 37, 42, 43, 44, 45, 46, 47, 48, 49, 50, 51, 52, 53, 54, 56, 57, 58/59, 66, 67, 68, 69, 70, 71, 72, 73, 74, 75, 76, 77, 78/79, 83, 84, 87, 88, 89, 90, 91, 92, 93, 95, 96, 97, 98, 99, 100, 101, 102, 103, 104, 105, 106, 107, 108, 109, 116, 118, 121, 122, 123, 124,125, 126,127,128, 130, 131, 132, 133, 134, 135, 136, 137, 138, 139, 140, 141, 142, 143, 144, 145, 146, 147, 148, 149, 150, 151, 152, 153, 154/155.
DaimlerChrysler Archive: 16 (b), 22 (r), 41, 55 (r), 59 (a), 59 (b), 62, 78 (l), 80, 81, 82, 84/85, 85 (r), 86.
Crash.net: 3, 164, 165, 166, 167, 168, 169, 170, 171, 172, 173, 174, 175.
Trevor Legate: 115, 117, 118/119, 120, 129.
Jackie Skelton/Exposure Images: 65.
Ferret Fotographics: 94.

100 YEARS OF
GRAND PRIX

Celebrating a Century of Grand Prix Racing 1906–2006

Trevor Legate

TOUCHSTONE
BOOKS LTD

HISTORIC GRAND PRIX CARS ASSOCIATION

The Historic Grand Prix Cars Association is delighted to add its support to this book, published to celebrate the centenary of Grand Prix racing.

The association, which was formed in 1979 with 75 members and has now grown to around 350, represents owners and drivers of cars that span almost half a century of racing, from 1925 to 1966. Our intention is to ensure that the two thousand cars at our disposal do not all languish idle within museums, but are seen by enthusiasts at race circuits around Europe, being driven and enjoyed. These cars recreate the special sounds and thrills of a wonderful period in the history of Grand Prix racing with wheel-to-wheel battles, four-wheel drifts through corners and a sporting camaraderie amongst the drivers that continues after the chequered flag.

Historic Grand Prix racing has seen a huge increase in popularity over recent years; when the races are over, spectators are more than welcome to inspect the cars, talk to the drivers and soak up an atmosphere that was commonplace before the sport became 'professional'.

Within the pages of this book, you will see many of 'our' cars racing in period, locked in battle and driven by some of the finest drivers the sport has seen. As president of the HGPCA, may I extend a cordial invitation to anyone with an interest in motor sport to visit one of the many race meetings we attend throughout the year, at such famous venues as Silverstone, Brands Hatch, Pau and the Nürburgring. The members of the HGPCA keep Grand Prix cars alive and welcome your support.

Sincerely
Richard Attwood
President, HGPCA

CONTENTS

FOREWORD

SIR JACKIE STEWART OBE

Formula One World Champion 1969 • 1971 • 1973

I first entered the world of Formula One Grand Prix racing on January 1st 1965, at the wheel of a BRM. The venue was South Africa and I well recall a fellow Scot by the name of Jim Clark being fastest in practice to take pole position in his Lotus and go on to win the race. Having just made the transition from Formula 3, I was more than delighted to collect a World Championship point when I finished in sixth place, and was even more delighted when I won the Italian Grand Prix at Monza seven races later.

Driving a Formula One car was, and undoubtedly still is, an intoxicating experience – a mixture of unconfined speed, total concentration and a desire to prove yourself to be the best amongst your peers. To drive a Formula One car at its absolute limit, while extending yourself to your own human limit, on a regular and consistent basis, is something very special. Such moments, gave me an adrenalin rush perhaps like no other. Little wonder that so many drivers during the past 100 years have found it difficult to walk away from an inherently dangerous sport. On too many occasions, they gave their lives doing what they loved most.

My personal experience highlighted the lack of skilled medical care within most of the sport in 1966. Being trapped in the cockpit of my car at Spa, soaked in petrol for twenty-five minutes, then being put onto the back of a hay truck before an ambulance could be found to cart me off to hospital, tends to focus the mind on the issue of safety and driver care. Having survived the experience, I was only too happy to speak my mind, even though not everyone agreed with my opinions, since track, spectator and driver protection costs money. I personally knew over 50 drivers who died while racing, but eventually common sense took over and logical precautions began to be established. Today, full medical facilities are taken for granted, but drivers raced for over sixty years with little cover. Grand Prix racing will never be free from accidents, but the record of fatalities is now very different. The last driver to die in a race was Ayrton Senna; more than ten years ago during a tragic weekend where another driver – Roland Ratzenberger, also lost his life, during the practice session. The last fatality in a race before that was twelve years earlier.

We now have Formula One cars that offer unprecedented levels of driver protection and the injury list is very different from my time, despite speeds having risen dramatically, as technology has created a new breed and generation of machine. Throughout the pages of this book are many emotive images that illustrate the development of the Grand Prix car from the first motorised carriages, shod with wooden artillery wheels, to the amazing Formula One cars of today, built from materials adapted from the aerospace industry and honed and shaped in wind tunnels. Aerodynamics is the new 'dark art' within the sport, as huge amounts of downforce push and pull the car onto the track, resulting in barely credible cornering speeds.

I consider myself extremely fortunate to have been able to experience motor racing at the highest level, and to leave without serious injury. I was privileged to compete against some of the best drivers to take part in the sport and witnessed huge changes in the sport during my nine seasons behind the wheel. In 1965, cars raced on narrow treaded tyres and had rudimentary bodywork but by 1973, I raced cars with huge slick, treadless tyres and briefly, the huge rear wing extensions that were the forerunners of the aerodynamic designs we now take for granted.

Having returned to the sport in 1997 as a Team Owner, I can say that I have experienced Grand Prix racing at every level; I have witnessed the fantastic highs and, occasionally, tragic lows. It is a sport that can be uplifting and exasperating – chasing those elusive hundredths of a second, whether as a driver or a Team Owner, can drive any sane person to the edge! But ultimately it is in our nature to compete against one another and to revel in the thrill of speed for its own sake. Grand Prix racing has dominated every aspect of my life; I have no regrets and offer my congratulations on its centenary, as well as wishing the current World Champion, Fernando Alonso, every success for the future, and the sport continued success for at least another 100 years.

INTRODUCTION

THE PIONEER YEARS

(1894–1905)

The most significant development in the creation of a self-propelled vehicle took place in 1885 when, at approximately the same time but quite independently, Karl Benz and Gottlieb Daimler introduced successful petrol-powered vehicles. Although the Benz tricycle was a more refined example of engineering, Daimler chose to add an engine to a four-wheeled carriage. This design proved to be more significant as both engineers developed the 'horseless-carriages' that eventually led to the creation of the automobile industry.

At the time, wealthy gentlemen raced horses, so inevitably it was not long before a competitive motor race was organized. Although Britain was at the forefront of the industrial revolution, and Germany was largely responsible for the internal combustion engine, neither country embraced the first horseless carriages. It was the French who appreciated the possibilities of the automobile and were the first to develop motor sport. The first automotive 'reliability' trial was organized by the French newspaper *Le Velocipede* in 1887. The event consisted of a short journey from Paris to Versailles but unfortunately only one adventurous competitor arrived at the start line, resulting in the world's first motor race being cancelled.

The first vehicles were decidedly expensive but gradually this new method of transport gained acceptance and in 1894 another French newspaper, *Le Petit Journal*, arranged another trial to take place between Paris and Rouen. This time 21 vehicles competed for a 5000-franc prize and each car was crewed by a driver and mechanic. The first vehicle home in this demanding race was a steam-powered tractor driven by the Count Jules de Dion who averaged 11.58mph for the 80-mile journey. However, since the organizers considered his vehicle to be outside the regulations, he had to forfeit the first prize.

In 1895, a race was organized in Italy and in November of that year, America joined in with a *Chicago Times-Herald* sponsored event that was contested between just two competitors. The race was won by Oscar Mueller, driving a Mueller-Benz, and the following year, seven competitors took part in another race held in New York.

It was soon apparent that motor sport was an effective method of advertising the automobile and in 1895 a consortium of Parisian newspaper publishers was formed with the intention of promoting the motor car. This group was later referred to as the 'Automobile Club de France' (ACF). The first event to be organized took place between Paris and Bordeaux and back. Emile Levassor drove virtually non-stop for 48 hours 48 minutes to take victory. Sadly his automobile had two seats rather than the stipulated four so he was denied the 31,000-franc prize, but history has been kinder as his statue overlooks the finish line at Port Malliot in Paris, in honour of his achievement.

The event was the first of numerous 'city-to-city' races that proved immensely popular as crowds gathered to line the route, cheering competitors as they battled over rough dirt roads. The events became more ambitious as, in 1896, the ACF organized a race of 950 miles from Paris to Marseilles and back, over a period of ten days; the winning Panhard covered the route in 67 hours 42 minutes. Motor sport was not without its inherent dangers and suffered its first fatality during the 1898 Paris-Nice event when Monsieur de Montariol waved to another competitor as he passed. He lost control and the car rolled over, killing his mechanic, while de Montariol died later from his injuries. Naturally this caused concern, especially amongst the Parisian authorities who tried to stop the Paris-Amsterdam-Paris race. This proved fruitless when the organizers started the race outside Paris and, at the end, a huge crowd turned out to cheer home the winning car. Eventually reliability trials were replaced by outright races and in 1899 the first Tour de France event took place over a 1272-mile route. Nineteen vehicles competed over several days with victory going to a Panhard. The era of the great city-to-city races came to an end in 1903 with the Paris-Madrid event. The French government stopped the race at Bordeaux by which time eight people had already died, including Marcel Renault. The increasingly powerful vehicles were often driven by over-enthusiastic and inexperienced gentlemen who discovered that the handling and braking abilities of their automobiles left much to be desired. The race had descended into carnage, leaving the authorities with little option but to ban racing on public roads.

A new series of races had been introduced in 1900 when an American newspaper tycoon, James Gordon Bennett, donated a trophy for an annual race. (At the time, he was based in Paris and was a founder member of the ACF). The trophy was to be contested by up to three representatives from each country and each vehicle had to conform to weight stipulations. Although the French representatives objected to the new rules, they relented when Bennett announced they would hold the first event in June 1900. Five automobiles contested the race between Paris and Lyon, which was won by a French driver, Fernand Charron in a Panhard 40. Since it was agreed that the winning country would host the following event, the 1901 Trophy race was held between Paris and Bordeaux. A French driver won, since he was the only person to complete the route.

The following year the 'Gordon Bennett Trophy' was held between Paris and Innsbruck and this gave Britain its first success in a major international race when the redoubtable Selwyn Francis Edge brought his Napier home in first place. The following year, the race was held in Ireland since road-racing was banned in England. Victory went to Camille Jenatzy, driving a Mercedes, which resulted in the race taking place in Germany in 1904. Leon Thery, driving a Richard-Brasier, fought off the challenge of Jenatzy to ensure the race returned to France for 1905 where he secured victory once again. Although France had won four of the six races, the continued objections regarding allowing just three competitors from each country caused Gordon Bennett to lose patience and transfer his allegiance from motor sport to ballooning, creating a Trophy race which continues to this day. The legendary races that he instigated were the first truly international motoring events and played a critical role in the development of the sport.

Motor sport was directly responsible for the rapid progress in both automobile development and the creation of better, more reliable combustion engines. By 1903, an American manufacturer, Winton, had created a huge eight-cylinder engine of 17 litres and Mercedes responded with a 21-litre engine that powered its land-speed record car, the Blitzen-Benz. Automobiles were built to establish numerous speed records and large sums of money were available to the successful entrants, especially in the USA where prestigious races such as the Vanderbilt Cup, held on Rhode Island, attracted the very best European cars and drivers. In Europe, the Coppa Florio was established in Italy from 1904 while Britain got around its road-racing restrictions by organizing the Tourist Trophy that took place on the Isle of Man in 1905. At the time, however, it was French cars and drivers that were dominant in the sport. At the instigation of the ACF, a race was organized to challenge the very best cars and drivers and, now that road races had been outlawed, this was arranged around a circuit of closed public roads and would carry the title 'Grand Prix'.

1 GREAT RACES AND GREAT HEROES

(1906–1927)

The first automobile race to be run as a 'Grand Prix' was held in France during 26th and 27th June 1906, using a closed circuit of some 60 miles arranged to the east of the town of Le Mans. In 1906 a motor race was a true test of endurance and reliability and the first Grand Prix was contested over a distance of 768 miles during the course of two days.

The race was arranged to replace the most important motoring event held in Europe, the Gordon Bennett Trophy that had been held annually between 1900 and 1905. This race was held on public roads between cities and had been initiated by a wealthy American newspaper proprietor, James Gordon Bennett, who was based in Paris. The regulations contained two major stipulations that would prove the downfall of the event; each country could enter no more than three cars and every component on the vehicle had to be made in the country of origin. In 1900 and 1901, only France entered and it was 1902 before any serious challenge emerged. However, the French sporting authority, the ACF, pressed to be allowed more than three entries to acknowledge its greater contribution. By 1905, the ACF lost patience and planned its own national race, a Grand Prix, and from 1906 Bennett transferred his allegiance to balloon racing (an event which continues to this day).

The new regulations permitted each manufacturer to enter up to three automobiles that conformed to a weight limit of 1000kg, excluding wings, lights, upholstery and tool kit. Exhausts had to run horizontally and were curved upwards at the rear to keep dust disturbance to a minimum. Every company of note rushed to enter; Renault, Fiat, Mercedes, Panhard and De Dietrich were amongst the entry list of 32 cars from 12 companies. The riding mechanic could be replaced at any time but the driver could only be replaced after the first day. Each lap of the roughly triangular circuit took about an hour to complete and was run over six laps each day.

The first car across the line on day one was the Renault of Hungarian driver Ferenc Szisz, followed by Frenchman Albert Clement in a Clement-Bayard with Felice Nazzaro's Fiat third. The last two drivers swapped positions on the second day but Szisz won again to secure overall victory. Much of his success was attributed to the new detachable wheel rim developed by Michelin that allowed the tyres to be changed in around three minutes instead of the usual 15. These 'jaute amovible' wooden artillery wheels contributed a great deal of weight but the time saved changing wheels made it worth fitting them. The Renault cars had another adaptation that helped on the very rough roads of the time, as they were the first to use hydraulic dampers that had been invented by Louis Renault. Of the 32 cars that started the Grand Prix, 11 survived, due in part to the intense heat of the weekend and the poorly resurfaced road that broke up as a result of the unusually hot weather.

1906 also saw the introduction of the Targa Florio, held on a long and dangerous circuit that wound around the island of Sicily. Although many of the mountainous roads had not been repaired for many hundreds of years, the Targa Florio continued, in various forms, into the 1970s. Such events were contested initially by the same cars that took part in Grand Prix events and played a crucial role in both the development of motor sport and the Grand Prix cars of the future. Ironically, 1906 would prove to be a watershed for the early domination of motor sport by the French since, over the next decade, the sport would become more organized and professional and Italian drivers would walk off with a greater share of the trophies. In fact 1907 saw Italian entries from Fiat, Isotta-Fraschini and Itala win the majority of the important races. Fiat became the most successful marque as automobile sales rose in proportion to its fame, and Felice Nazzaro became a household name.

The concept of the Grand Prix had still to be established in other European countries, although a race was organized each year in America under the 'Grand Prix' title. In Germany the national motor sport club (ADAC) held the first of a series of Kaiserpreis races for touring cars and a similar race was established in Italy, the Coppa Florio. In 1907, both the German and Italian races, plus the French Grand Prix, were won by Felice Nazzaro in a Fiat. The Grand Prix was held in Dieppe, run to a revised set of rules that were based around fuel consumption in an effort to stem the growth in engine capacity. The industry was becoming concerned that the racing cars of the time had little in common with the road-going automobiles they were trying to sell.

Even though British drivers enjoyed a reasonable level of success in Europe, the UK government continued to resist the call for motor sport to take place on public roads, to the detriment of its motor industry. In an effort to improve the situation, Hugh Locke-King and a group of wealthy friends combined forces to build a race circuit on land that he owned in Surrey. The result was the impressive Brooklands track, a huge concrete oval with high-banked corners. The work was completed in 1907 and the first purpose-built racing circuit was unveiled – and it did not go unnoticed in other countries!

In 1908, the ACF Grand Prix remained in Dieppe but the rules changed once again, this time with a minimum weight limit (1100kg) and a maximum bore size for the engine. The impressive Mercedes of Christian Lautenschlager took victory ahead of two other entries from Benz & Co. However, from 1909 a serious economic depression affected the motor industry in Europe. When the ACF changed the regulations for the 1909 French Grand Prix, the manufacturers had no hesitation in cancelling their entries and the race was not held again until 1911. One of the major casualties of the withdrawal was Renault who would not return to Grand Prix racing until 1977. In the USA, racing continued and in 1909 the Indianapolis Motor Speedway followed the Brooklands lead and opened to great acclaim since it provided close and competitive racing and the spectators could see the entire circuit. Even better, the crowds could be kept apart from the cars and the organizers could charge an entry fee.

The ACF succeeded in holding another Grand Prix in 1912 by allowing virtually any type of car to compete. Victory went to a Frenchman, Georges Boillot, driving a Peugeot L76 and victory was secured by Peugeot the following year. However, it was evident that war in Europe was a real possibility and motor racing was dragged into the conflict as national governments tried to use it for political ends. Matters came to a head at the infamous French Grand Prix of 1914, often referred to as the Race of The Century, which was held at a circuit near Lyon on July 5th. Of the 37 cars entered, five came from Mercedes who took on three cars from Peugeot. One of the Mercedes was driven by Max Sailer who was a director of the company, and he led the race initially before engine problems allowed Georges Boillot to pass. On lap 17, Christian Lautenschlager inherited the lead in his Mercedes as two other Mercedes moved into third and fourth. On the final lap, the engine of Boillot's battered Peugeot, that had been driven to its very limit, overheated and Mercedes took a 1-2-3 victory. The prize-giving took place in near silence and photographs of the winning cars and their laurel wreaths were sent around the world to glorify the victory. The race proved to be the final major sporting event before war broke out.

It was 1921 before another Grand Prix could be organized. During the First World War, almost all the Grand Prix cars were transferred to the USA, where the American automobile manufacturers had an opportunity to inspect them. A number of top drivers decided to continue racing and also spent the war years in America. The damage done to the sport during the seven-year hiatus was highlighted by the domination of the 1921 French Grand Prix by a team of cars from Duesenberg that crossed the Atlantic to take on the European automobiles. The race was won by a talented Irish-American driver, Jimmy Murphy, in a 3-litre Duesenberg, to the surprise of the European companies. However, a great deal of new technology had been developed in a short period of time during the war years and the car manufacturers soon introduced supercharged engines and overhead camshafts to the sport. New cars from Fiat, Alfa Romeo and Sunbeam became more sophisticated than the relatively crude American automobiles. Not just the cars, but the circuits also changed as smaller, permanent tracks,

such as Monza, were built around Europe. Italy became the first country other than France to host a Grand Prix, followed by Belgium and Spain in 1924, although the races remained an informal collection of events run to a variety of regulations. Since cars no longer travelled long distances, the riding mechanic became superfluous and was banned from 1925. That year saw the introduction of a World Championship comprising of four races to be held in Italy, Spain, Belgium, as Grand Prix, and the USA where the Indianapolis 500 was included. The championship was fought between the manufacturers, not the drivers, and Alfa Romeo took the first title. The French dominance may have been suppressed, but it was not finished as Bugatti took the championship in 1926, followed by Delage in 1927.

Above: Where it all began: the winning Renault of Ferenc Szisz at the first Grand Prix, Le Mans 1906. The Renault averaged over 100kph during the race and won by over half an hour. Although the 95 horsepower automobile had less power than many of its rivals, it used removable wheel rims held in place by eight bolts. This allowed faster tyre changes and the mechanic, M. Marteau, was kept busy throughout the race as the rough roads caused punctures on a regular basis. Szisz joined Renault in 1900 and progressed to take charge of the test department before being appointed the chief race driver for the company. His victory at the Grand Prix brought him considerable fame and he became a household name in France.

Below: The Itala of Pierre de Caters at the ACF Grand Prix, 1906. The Italian-built car had a 25hp advantage over the winning Renault, but tyre changes took ten minutes longer. Both driver and his riding mechanic were totally exposed to the elements and suffered burns from the tar mixture (a forerunner of asphalt) that had been spread on the roads and melted in the heat. Cars were identified by letters and numbers – this Itala was 8C while the winning Renault was 3A. Unfortunately, all three Italas retired before the end of the first day.

Left: The Renault team prior to the start of the 1907 ACF Grand Prix held in Dieppe. (Left to right: Ferenc Szisz, Henry Farman, Claude Richez) Szisz was expected to win again but due to concerns about fuel consumption, he ran a conservative race, finishing just seven minutes behind the winning Fiat of Felice Nazzaro after almost 500 miles of racing. After the event, it was discovered that the Renault still had a considerable amount of fuel in the tank. The Renault of Richez finished in 13th place while Farman retired after seven of the ten laps.

Above: The winning Fiat of Felice Nazzaro is refuelled during the 1907 ACF Grand Prix. Racecars of the period used chain drive and wooden artillery wheels. Note the two spare wheels mounted on the rear of the car, ready for the inevitable puncture. A typical tyre change took around 15 minutes and the hard-working mechanics earned their keep, not just having to change wheels but also pumping fuel to the engine and checking components whilst racing.

Above: The Fiat of Felice Nazzaro en route to victory in the ACF Grand Prix 1907. The race was open to a maximum of three cars from each manufacturer and 11 entries were received from France with one each from Italy, Britain, Belgium, Germany and the USA. A French victory was considered a certainty and it was a shock when an Italian automobile came home in first place. The Renault of Szisz was a firm favourite and might have won had he not slowed to conserve fuel, although he was just seven minutes behind after 6 hours 46 minutes of racing.

Opposite: By the time of the 1908 French (ACF) Grand Prix, once again held in Dieppe, the white Mercedes cars from the Daimler factory were a force to be reckoned with. Victory went to Christian Lautenschlager with team mate Willy Poge in fifth place. The Mercedes of Otto Salzer retired having set the fastest lap of the race on lap 2. The Renault of Ferenc Szisz retired whilst lying in third place and the Fiat team succumbed to technical problems, dropping out by the third lap. Two other German cars from the Benz factory finished second and third.

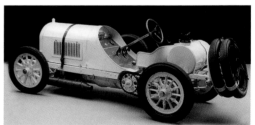

Above: The 1908 Grand Prix car from Benz & Cie had a 15-litre four-cylinder engine that produced 158bhp.

Above: The Grand Prix was not held in France during 1909 and 1910 so events such as the Targa Florio came into their own. In 1910, the fourth running of the Targa Florio in Sicily attracted a small entry and proved the ideal venue for the small, lightweight 'voiturette' Lion-Peugeot cars entered by the French Autos et Cycles Peugeot company. Their voiturettes beat the larger-capacity cars to take the first three places after racing for 5 hours 20 minutes over two laps of the full 92.4-mile Madonie circuit. The photograph shows the winning car of Georges Boillot and two other Lion-Peugeots finished in second and third places driven by Giosue Giuppone and Jules Goux.

Right: In 1911 the French Grand Prix was revived and run over 12 laps of the Le Mans circuit, a distance of 655 kilometres. The only car to complete the full distance was the Fiat of French driver Victor Hémery, with a Bugatti in second place and another French automobile, a Rolland-Pilain, third. The photograph shows another Rolland-Pilain that was driven by Victor Rigal who was classified in eighth place despite having retired on the fifth lap.

Left: The 1912 ACF Grand Prix (officially titled the XII Grand Prix de l'Automobile Club de France – the French counted the inter-city Gordon Bennett trophy races from 1900 as Grand Prix) took place in Dieppe over the 25th-26th June. As the small-engined voiturettes were permitted to enter, a total of 47 cars did battle on dirt roads over a distance of 1,535 kilometres and the race was won by the Peugeot L-76 of Georges Boillot, car number 22. He finished ten minutes ahead of the Fiat S74 of Louis Wagner, followed by three voiturette Sunbeams. The winning car completed the race in 13 hours 58 minutes at an average speed of 110.16kph.

Opposite: With the threat of war hanging over the 1914 French Grand Prix, emotions were running high and cars from German manufacturers were hardly welcome. The huge crowds cheered on the three-car Peugeot team but disaster struck on the penultimate lap when the engine of Georges Boillot's Peugeot expired while in second place. This allowed the Mercedes team to cruise to a 1-2-3 victory that was not well received by the patriotic French spectators. The photograph shows the third-place Mercedes of Otto Salzer who finished behind his team mates Christian Lautenschlager and Louis Wagner.

Below: A new formula for Grand Prix cars was devised in September 1913, regulating the engines to 4.5 litres and weighing less than 1100kg (2425lb). This rule helped Vauxhall, Sunbeam and especially Peugeot, who were firm favourites to win the now infamous 1914 French Grand Prix. The five cars from Mercedes were not considered a serious threat but after a dramatic race involving the Peugeot of Georges Boillot, Mercedes finished in the first three places. The photograph shows the Mercedes of Otto Salzer who finished third. The victorious Mercedes of Christian Lautenschlager was sent to Britain to promote Daimler but when war broke out, it was impounded and sent to Rolls Royce in Derby where the Maybach-designed engine was stripped and inspected. This became the template for all Rolls Royce aero engines during the First World War.

Opposite: Grand Prix racing resumed in 1921 with the ACF-organized event held at Le Mans. The French Ballot team fully expected one of its three drivers to win but it was in for a surprise. The race was won by a Duesenberg but in second place was a privately entered Ballot that had been shipped from America for its owner Ralph de Palma (shown here). He was joined by his nephew, Peter de Paolo, who served as his riding mechanic. M. Ballot did all he could to ensure one of his drivers would win, but despite being given an under-powered engine, de Palma drove a conservative race to finish six minutes ahead of the third-placed Ballot of Jules Goux.

Left: While European Grand Prix motor racing suffered a seven-year hiatus, the sport thrived in America. When racing resumed in Europe in 1921, Duesenberg shipped a car to Le Mans to take part in the ACF Grand Prix, driven by the brilliant Irish-American Jimmy Murphy. He suffered a huge accident in practice when his car rolled, but discharged himself from hospital just hours before the race. Swathed in bandages, he drove the 322 miles in 4 hours 7 minutes at an average speed of 79mph to win the race. Instead of celebrating the amazing act of skill and courage, his success was snubbed by the race organizers and Murphy walked out of the victory party to find a restaurant. Jimmy Murphy died in 1924, but was the only American driver to win a Grand Prix and the Indianapolis 500 until Mario Andretti equalled the feat. He won at Indy in 1969 and celebrated his first GP victory, the South African, in 1971.

Opposite: The 1922 ACF Grand Prix took place over 60 laps of a 13.38 kilometre circuit in Strasbourg, close to the Bugatti factory. All cars had to comply to a 2-litre formula with two seater bodywork and a dry weight of 650kg. Four of the new cigar-shaped Bugatti Type 29s were entered but the experienced Felice Nazzaro (shown here in car number 4) brought his Fiat 804 home almost an hour ahead of the Bugattis of Pierre De Vizcaya and Pierre Marco. It was his last victory, but it was tarnished by the tragic death of his nephew, Biagio Nazzaro, who was killed when the rear axle of his Fiat collapsed at maximum speed on one of the long, fast straights.

Left: The 1922 French (ACF) Grand Prix proved unsuccessful for the Rolland-Pilain A22 of Victor Hemery and the cars of his two team mates, who all retired in a race of attrition; only three cars survived the full 60 laps. By now, cars were lower and lighter and made use of wire wheels. Bodywork was becoming more streamlined although it would be many years before technology permitted a greater understanding of aerodynamics.

Above: While Grand Prix racing was becoming established in Europe, road racing in Britain still had to take place away from the mainland. The 1922 Tourist Trophy was held on the Isle of Man and the open-category 'Formula Libre' race was won by a Sunbeam driven by a Frenchman, Jean Chassagne. More British manufacturers were building cars for competition use by now and the event was contested by Vauxhall, Bentley and Sunbeam. Fourth place went to a Bentley driven by W.O. Bentley.

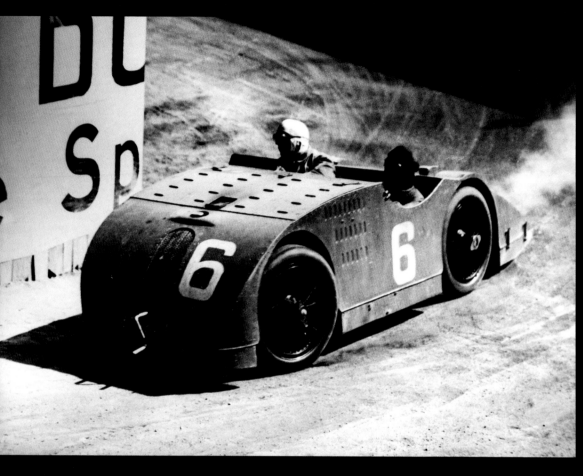

Opposite: The 1923 French Grand Prix saw the introduction of supercharged engines and some radical bodywork designs. As well as the Bugatti 'Tank', aviation pioneer and automobile constructor Gabriel Voisin arrived with exotic-looking Voisin Laboratoires. He had hoped the aerodynamic bodywork would compensate for the lack of power from the relatively unsophisticated sleeve-valve engine, but it was not to be. One Voisin, driven by André Lefèbvre, finished the race in fifth place, one hour and 15 minutes behind Henry Segrave's Sunbeam, while the Voisin in the photograph, driven by Andre Morel, was disqualified.

Above: The 1923 ACF Grand Prix took place in Tours and saw the arrival of four of Bugatti's short-wheelbase Type 32, referred to for obvious reasons, as the 'Tank'. Ernest Friderich fought to prevent a clean-sweep by the British Sunbeams and managed to bring his Bugatti home in third place behind the Sunbeams of Henry Segrave and Albert Divo. The slab-sided Bugattis were an early exercise in streamlining and were radically different in appearance to any other Grand Prix car. Each featured an eight-cylinder overhead camshaft engine with a capacity of 1991cc that produced around 90 horsepower. Sadly, the Type 32 suffered from instability at speed and poor roadholding, while the driver and mechanic sat with their legs beside the hot engine. Ettore Bugatti returned home after the race to reconsider the problem and his solution for the 1924 season was to create one of the most successful racing cars of all time – the Type 35.

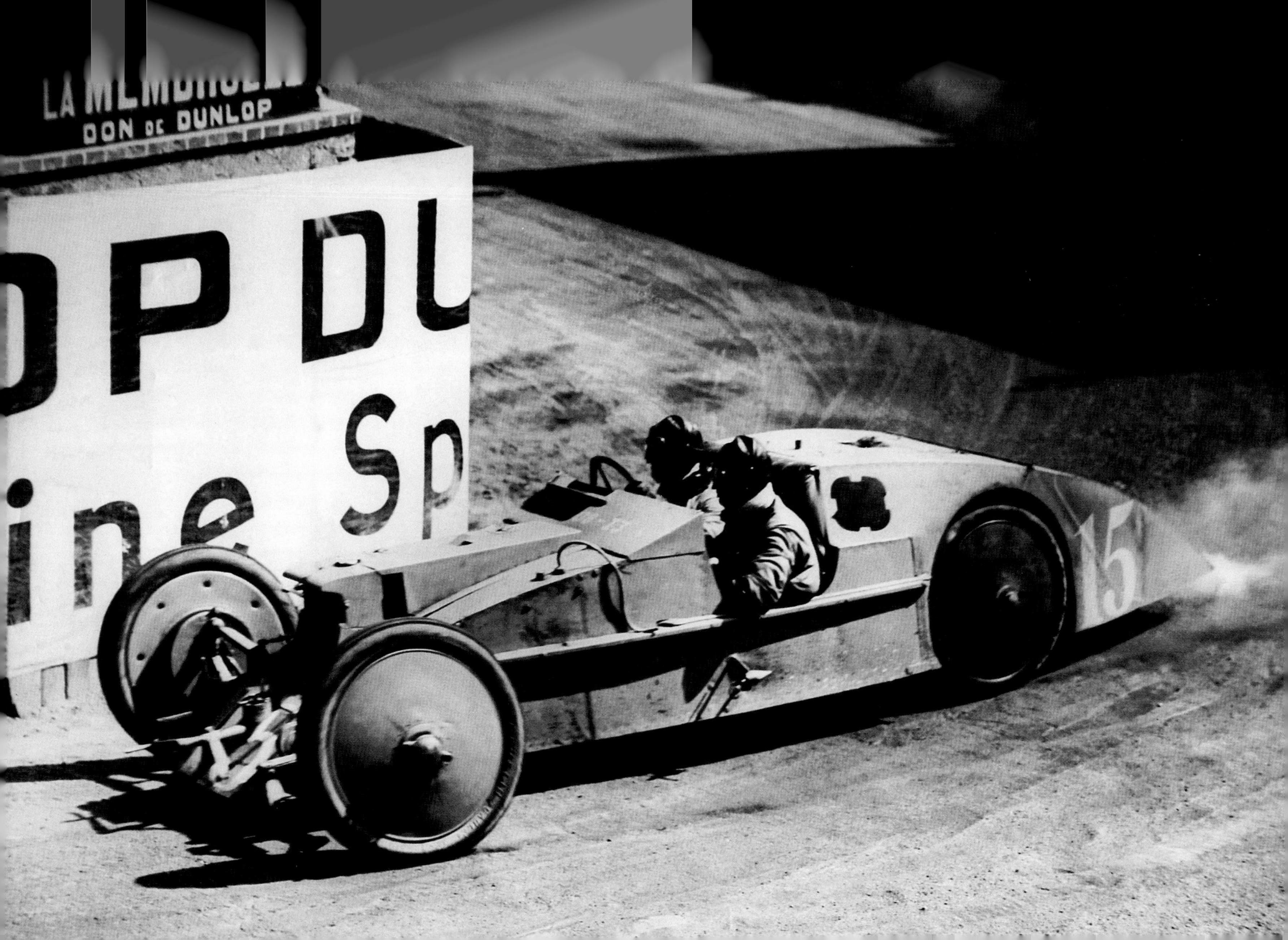
DON DE DUNLOP
OP DU
ine Sp
15

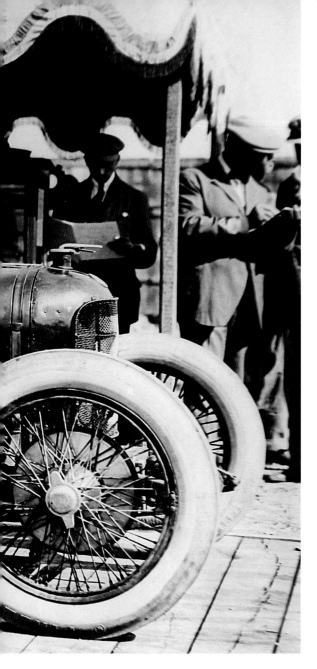

Left: The 1924 ACF Grand Prix took place in Lyon on August 3rd. The competition was becoming more intense as new and revised cars arrived from Delage, Bugatti and Alfa Romeo in an effort to halt the domination of the British Sunbeams. The new Bugatti Type 35s showed promise but the beautiful P2 (8C/2000) model from Alfa Romeo took victory in its first season as Giuseppe Campari came home ahead of the Delages, with Louis Wagner fourth in another Alfa Romeo. Grand Prix continued to be run over considerable distances, in this case 35 laps of a circuit around Lyon, a distance of 815 kilometres and lasting over seven hours. One driver who was scheduled to drive an Alfa Romeo, but did not start, would play an increasingly important role in Grand Prix history – Enzo Ferrari.

Above: Although the crowd seem intent on inspecting another vehicle at the 1924 ACF Grand Prix, the Delage 2LCV of Robert Benoist was an important development in race car design and capable of giving the successful Alfa Romeo P2 a hard time. The 2LCV was raced between 1923, when Delage returned to racing, and 1925 with engines that offered between 116 and 205 horsepower. The remarkable four overhead camshaft V12 engine produced more power than the chassis could handle when a supercharger was used in 1923, but ran without one for much of 1924. This image also illustrates how narrow tyres were during the 1920s. Benoist brought Delage number 9 home in third place ahead of an Alfa Romeo P2 but behind the winning P2 of Campari and the Delage of Albert Divo.

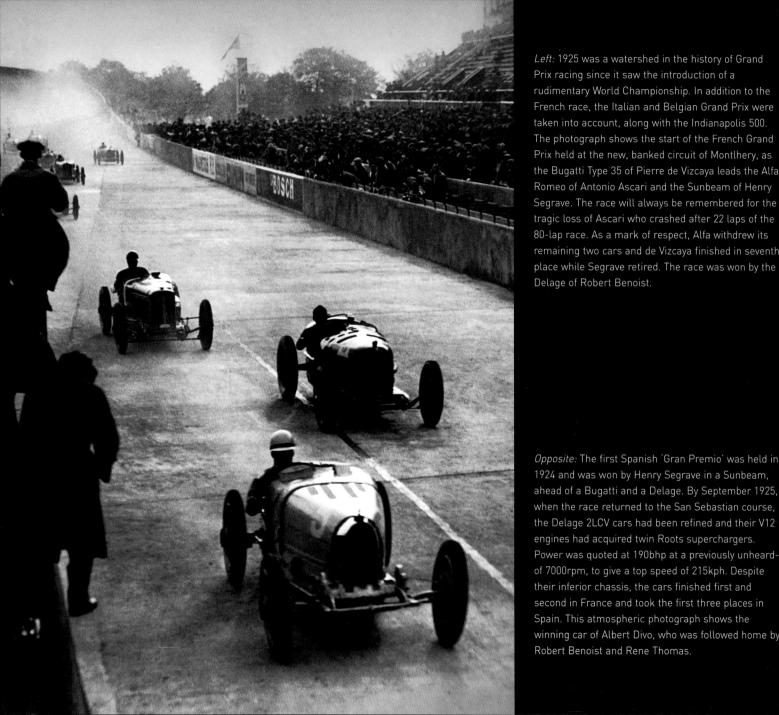

Left: 1925 was a watershed in the history of Grand Prix racing since it saw the introduction of a rudimentary World Championship. In addition to the French race, the Italian and Belgian Grand Prix were taken into account, along with the Indianapolis 500. The photograph shows the start of the French Grand Prix held at the new, banked circuit of Montlhery, as the Bugatti Type 35 of Pierre de Vizcaya leads the Alfa Romeo of Antonio Ascari and the Sunbeam of Henry Segrave. The race will always be remembered for the tragic loss of Ascari who crashed after 22 laps of the 80-lap race. As a mark of respect, Alfa withdrew its remaining two cars and de Vizcaya finished in seventh place while Segrave retired. The race was won by the Delage of Robert Benoist.

Opposite: The first Spanish 'Gran Premio' was held in 1924 and was won by Henry Segrave in a Sunbeam, ahead of a Bugatti and a Delage. By September 1925, when the race returned to the San Sebastian course, the Delage 2LCV cars had been refined and their V12 engines had acquired twin Roots superchargers. Power was quoted at 190bhp at a previously unheard-of 7000rpm, to give a top speed of 215kph. Despite their inferior chassis, the cars finished first and second in France and took the first three places in Spain. This atmospheric photograph shows the winning car of Albert Divo, who was followed home by Robert Benoist and Rene Thomas.

Left: Born in 1874, the extrovert Louis Delage was a gentleman of modest means, but when he eventually acquired a considerable amount of money, he was not afraid to spend it. He created his own automobile manufacturing company in 1905 to become part of the exciting new industry. Delage entered Grand Prix racing in 1913 with the intention of producing the fastest automobiles in the world. Following the First World War, the company returned to Grand Prix events in 1923 and its finest year was 1927, when the 155B, shown here outside the Delage factory, proved unbeatable in European races. At the end of 1927, Delage decided it had nothing more to prove and to stem the crippling expense of competing, the race team was disbanded. The Great Depression of the 1930s saw the end of the Delage business and Louis Delage died in near poverty in 1947.

Opposite: For the 1926 season, Grand Prix regulations changed once again and cars now used engines of 1.5-litres capacity. Delage designed a remarkable, but very expensive, straight-eight engine which swept to victory the following year to win the World Championship and four of the five Grand Prix. Robert Benoist, in Delage number 6, is shown at the 1927 Gran Premio de Espana in San Sebastian, where he recorded a hard-fought victory over the Bugatti team. Benoist also won in France, Italy and Britain during the same year.

Right: In the 1927 ACF Grand Prix, held at Montlhery, the Delage automobiles over-ran the challenge of Bugatti. The previous year, 1926, had witnessed the embarrassing scene of just three cars starting the race (all Bugatti Type 39s) as only Bugatti had entered when the entry list closed. The Delages were not ready, along with many other potential entrants, but the organizers forgot to include a condition in the regulations that would allow them to cancel the race if insufficient entries had been received. It was probably the poorest Grand Prix ever witnessed (at least until 2005). It was a different story in 1927, even though Bugatti withdrew all five of its cars and the Delage 155Bs swept to a 1-2-3 victory, with Robert Benoist driving the winning car.

2 THE FORMULA LIBRE YEARS

(1928–1939)

Grand Prix racing had previously been conducted in accordance with a set of rules based around engine size and vehicle weight. By 1928, race organizers had abandoned the AIACR (Association Internationale des Automobiles Clubs – Recconus) regulation that stipulated the car could weigh no more than 550-600 kilograms, plus races should last a minimum distance of 600 kilometres. This resulted in Grand Prix being run to Formula Libre (free formula) rules and brought about a return of private entrants who owned older Grand Prix cars such as Bugattis, Delages and Talbots. It was the Bugatti Type 35B that dominated the major races, although the Alfa Romeo and the new Maserati teams shared some of the spoils for a few glorious years.

1929 saw the introduction of a Grand Prix held around the narrow streets of Monaco. The tiny principality made a rather unlikely race circuit but the sheer glamour of the location ensured its survival into the modern era. The first Monaco Grand Prix coincided with the start of the Mille Miglia, so Alfa Romeo split its entry between the two events, while Ettore Bugatti decided that Monte Carlo would be the ideal venue to display his products and, as a result, half the field consisted of Bugattis. Mercedes-Benz sent a 7.1-litre SSK for Rudolph Caracciola, who was a strong favourite for victory, but an Anglo-French amateur driver had other ideas. Charles Frederick William Grover-Williams was born in Paris and lived and worked in Monaco. He entered the race in his green Bugatti under the pseudonym, 'W. Williams', and, thanks in part to a slow pit stop by the Mercedes team, he managed to stay ahead of Caracciola to win.

Bugatti and 'Williams' also won the 1929 French Grand Prix while Bugatti also broke the Mercedes domination of the German Grand Prix. Alfa Romeo scored several notable victories on home soil. Motor sport was hugely popular during this period, not only Grand Prix events, but thanks in part to the success of a British team of drivers, the 'Bentley Boys', a group of wealthy enthusiasts who enjoyed considerable success in the Le Mans 24-Hours for a number of years, finishing in the first four places in 1929. In the same year, over 500,000 spectators lined the Ards circuit in Ireland to witness Caracciola win the Ulster TT in his Mercedes.

During 1930, after years of working for Alfa Romeo, Enzo Ferrari established his own racing team, Scuderia Ferrari, and negotiated a deal to run the racing department on behalf of Alfa Romeo. In Germany, Daimler-Benz felt the effects of an economic slump during the late 1920s and pulled out of racing during 1930, although team manager Alfred Neubauer succeeded in finding enough money to allow Caracciola to continue as a 'private' entrant.

The proposed fuel consumption formula was generally ignored by race promoters during 1931. They opted for a minimum race length of ten hours with two drivers sharing each car. This was adopted at the French, Italian and Belgian Grand Prix. Bugatti entered its Type 54 and Alfa developed the first true single-seat Grand Prix car, the Tipo A Monoposto. Bugatti won four of the six Grand Prix, Alfa Romeo won at Monza while the German Grand Prix was run to sports car rules that enabled Caracciola to win with his Mercedes SSK. The French Grand Prix celebrated its 25th anniversary with a lunch hosted for the drivers who won the first two races, Francois Szisz (1906) and Felice Nazzaro (1907). The race at Montlhery was won by Louis Chiron and Achille Varzi in a Bugatti that covered 782 miles in ten hours.

Alfa Romeo launched its elegant Vittorio Jano-designed P3 in 1932 and Caracciola was signed to drive for the team, since Mercedes could no longer afford to support his unofficial racing. He went on to win in Germany while

Tazio Nuvolari recorded victories at Monza, Monaco and Reims. Bugatti struggled to compete, winning only once at the Czech Grand Prix with Louis Chiron at the wheel.

In 1933, Alfa Romeo withdrew its monoposto P3 cars due to spiralling costs and falling sales. Scuderia Ferrari continued to race using older Alfa Monzas driven by Nuvolari and Borzacchini, while Caracciola formed another team of Monzas in partnership with Louis Chiron, who had been fired by Bugatti. Giuseppe Campari continued racing with his Maserati 8C 2800 while the only official works team was Bugatti who employed Achille Varzi, Albert Divo, Rene Dreyfus and William Grover-Williams. At the 1933 Monaco Grand Prix, a small piece of history was made when, at the suggestion of a journalist, the cars formed on the grid according to the times recorded in practice, instead of by ballot. This was a novel idea at the time, but has been adopted ever since. Varzi won the race in his Bugatti Type 51, but Nuvolari responded with a win in Germany. Campari won the French race at Montlhery and Nuvolari retired in Spain and Reims, which prompted him to change allegiance to Maserati. He then won the Belgian Grand Prix with a typical virtuoso performance, before he and Borzacchini decided to form their own team using the new Maserati 8CM monoposto. They were replaced at Scuderia Ferrari by Chiron and Luigi Fagioli while Enzo Ferrari persuaded Alfa Romeo to release its P3 to compete against Nuvolari. The two Scuderia drivers shared the victories between them, with Fagioli winning the important Italian Grand Prix, relegating Nuvolari to second place. This was a day of tragedy since later the same day, the Monza Grand Prix was held over two heats and a final. During the first heat, a quantity of oil was deposited onto the track and during the second heat, Campari and Borzacchini braked heavily while battling for the lead and left the circuit with fatal results. Both men were national heroes and Campari had announced his intention to retire following the race to continue his career as an opera singer (he was famous for singing arias whilst racing). In the final race of the day, Count Czaykowski lost control of his Bugatti at the same corner and was also killed. The era of the Formula Libre cars came to an end in tragic circumstances, since it had been agreed that, between 1934 and 1937, cars

would have to conform to a new formula that limited weight to 750kg, although engine capacity remained free.

In Germany, the ruling party decided to promote the superiority of German engineering through motor sport and offered a fund of £45,000 for companies prepared to build Grand Prix cars. Both Daimler-Benz and Auto Union accepted the challenge and designed a series of technologically advanced cars that would dominate the sport until 1939. From their first Grand Prix appearance at the Nürburgring in July 1934, when Hans Stuck won in his Auto Union Type A, the Italian manufacturers realized that their cars had been consigned to history. Not only did the Daimler-Benz and Auto Union cars look far more advanced, they made use of the new light alloys and each developed four-wheel independent suspension. While the Mercedes cars made use of a straight-eight engine mounted ahead of the driver, Auto Union went to Dr. Ferdinand Porsche's company and took over his rear-engine race car project. Without any engine restrictions and the availability of light alloys, Grand Prix cars became faster than ever. The Mercedes W25 of 1934 to 1936 produced 345 horsepower, enough to give a top speed of 175mph. However, the engines required the use of special highly flammable fuel, a lethal cocktail consisting primarily of methyl alcohol, and disposed of it at little more than 1mpg. Thus the drivers sat on top of 75-gallon unprotected fuel tanks as they travelled at ever greater speeds.

The new German cars first appeared at the Avus circuit in May 1934, in front of a patriotic crowd. The Mercedes-Benz team manager, Alfred Neubauer, had promised Rudi Caracciola a place in any future Mercedes team and he kept his word despite Caracciola being unfit due to a leg injury. He was joined by the German aristocrat, Manfred von Brauchitsch and the volatile Italian, Luigi Fagioli. Hans Stuck led the Auto Union team and Varzi, Chiron and Guy Moll drove the Alfa Romeos of Scuderia Ferrari. Matters did not go to plan for the Mercedes team since Neubauer did not consider the cars were fully race-prepared and took the difficult decision to withdraw rather than face a series of embarrassing retirements. The Auto Union of Hans Stuck built a commanding lead before clutch failure allowed Alfa Romeo to finish first and second. The Mercedes cars were ready for the next race, the Eifelrennen, two weeks later but they fell foul of the race scrutineers who discovered the cars were one kilogram over the weight limit. Neubauer decided the easiest solution was to strip off the paint, which achieved the weight target, and the cars raced with a light coating of aluminium paint over the bodywork. This resulted in a comment in the press reports, describing the cars as 'Silver Arrows', a popular description that was applied to all future Mercedes racing cars. In the race, the Mercedes W25s dominated but it seemed likely that victory would go to Fagioli, an unacceptable occurrence on German soil, so Neubauer ordered him to move over and allow von Brauchitsch to take the victory. He followed the order but engaged in a furious argument with Neubauer during a pit stop. Fagioli chased after von Brauchitsch and harassed him relentlessly before Neubauer called him into the pits again and the argument continued. To register his protest, Fagioli left the pits and parked his car at the side of the circuit to deny Mercedes a 1-2 finish, handing second place to Auto Union.

Mercedes-Benz was predominant during 1935, winning five of the nine major Grand Prix with Caracciola the most successful driver. Auto Union introduced a new driver of considerable talent, Bernd Rosemeyer, but the finest example of driving skill was given by Tazio Nuvolari in an Alfa Romeo P3 when he defeated the German teams in their own backyard, at the German Grand Prix. In spite of his car giving away over 100 horsepower to the Mercedes W25, Nuvolari put on an unforgettable demonstration of driving over 22 laps of the Nürburgring, moving steadily from sixth place to second after 14 laps, two minutes behind the Mercedes of Manfred von Brauchitsch. Convinced that he had an unassailable lead, von Brauchitsch slowed to preserve his car and tyres, but his earlier pace had already caused serious tyre wear. As Nuvolari rapidly closed the gap, von Brauchitsch was forced to drive faster, which caused a tyre to explode and Nuvolari went on to win. He defeated the Auto Union of Hans Stuck by over two minutes, after one of the most impressive drives ever witnessed, finishing ahead of nine state-of-the-art German cars in a four-year old Alfa Romeo.

This was a time of remarkable engineering progress as Auto Union succeeded in installing a 6006cc engine that produced 520bhp, in a car weighing only 750kg. The V12-engined Alfa Romeos were no match for the German cars even though, with Nuvolari at the wheel, anything was possible. Auto Union began to get the upper hand over Mercedes and Neubauer withdrew his cars before the end of the 1936 season to prevent further defeats and concentrated on preparing for 1937, when it unveiled the W125 with a straight-eight 5.6-litre engine that gave 575 horsepower, a figure not equalled in Grand Prix racing until 1981. In the hands of Rudolph Caracciola, the combination was virtually unbeatable, even though the Mercedes and Auto Union cars were now evenly matched. The cars were so fast, it would be another 20 years before Grand Prix cars could match their lap times. Away from the race track, the power of the new engines was enough to propel a streamlined Auto Union to a new speed record of 248.5mph on one of Germany's autobahns. In Britain, there was greater interest in establishing land speed records than winning Grand Prix races; George Eyston drove his 4,700 horsepower 'Thunderbolt' to 312mph on the Bonneville Salt Flats, raising it to 357mph in 1938. However, the British public were able to witness the new German cars they had read so much about when a Grand Prix was organized at Donington Park during October 1937. Betting was permitted at race tracks at the time and a lot of money was placed on such local drivers as Raymond Mays with his ERA, since his knowledge of the circuit was considered a great advantage. The entry consisted of five ERAs, two Maseratis and one Riley to confront the four Mercedes and three Auto Unions, but when the spectators witnessed the first practice laps of the German cars, they realized that the rumours had been far from exaggerated. The silver cars were visibly faster than the ERAs, hurtling through the corners in huge sideways drifts, smoke pouring from the tyres and the cars literally taking off over some the crests around Donington. They were reaching 170mph on the straight, speeds never before witnessed in England. The British fans were left almost speechless as the cars thundered around the track, the first four cars lapping the fastest British ERA by the end of lap four. In fact only five cars classified as finishers since the opposition was unable to complete a sufficient number of laps. Rosemeyer won for Auto Union ahead of the Mercedes W125s of von Brauchitsch and

Caracciola. The visit of the German teams to Donington passed into legend and nobody who attended that day would ever forget the spectacle, nor the sound and the fury of the cars; British motor sport now knew that Grand Prix racing in Europe was at a different level.

Although Nuvolari tried as only he could during 1937, his Alfa Romeo could not match the might of Mercedes-Benz and Auto Union. He accepted the offer to drive an Auto Union at the Swiss Grand Prix, if only to point out that he had other options. Alfa Romeo decided to bring the racing team back under its control by purchasing 80 per cent of Scuderia Ferrari, but allowed Enzo Ferrari to continue as racing manager. Political intrigue and arguments did little to help its cause and matters deteriorated when its new 158 Alfetta arrived during August 1937. Alfa took full control of the project via its own Alfa Corse team, but matters did not improve when the chassis was found to be weak which resulted in the factory firing its most capable engineer, Vittorio Jano. Worse was to follow when Alfa Romeo lost the services of Nuvolari after the first race of 1938, at Pau, where the fuel tank split and he received serious burns from the spilt fuel. He swore never to drive for Alfa Romeo again and joined Auto Union. The year began badly when the unofficial champion driver, Bernd Rosemeyer, lost his life whilst attempting to set a new speed record on an autobahn.

1938 saw the end of the futile 750kg limit and Grand Prix cars now complied with the new regulations of 3-litre supercharged or 4.5-litre atmospheric engines. Only Delahaye and Talbot opted for the latter as the new Mercedes W154 dominated in the hands of Caracciola and Hermann Lang, although Nuvolari won the final two Grand Prix of the year. The story was the same for 1939 as a full season of racing was scheduled in spite of the unstable political climate in Europe. The Mercedes W154 remained the most competitive Grand Prix car, despite the arrival of the new Auto Union Type D. Alfa Romeo remained outclassed, Maserati still suffered financial problems and Bugatti concentrated on sports car racing. To guarantee an Italian victory at the Tripoli Grand Prix, the Italian organizers announced that the race would be run as a 1.5-litre 'voiturette' race, certain that the German teams did not have a suitable car or engine. However, they seriously underestimated Mercedes-Benz. In just eight months, the company designed and built a car that was powered by a 1.5-litre V8 engine and was completed just in time to run in Tripoli in May 1939. (Auto Union also undertook construction of a suitable car, since it was generally assumed that the 1.5-litre limit might be adopted from 1940, but they missed the deadline). The Mercedes W165, driven by Hermann Lang, scored a remarkable victory in the brand new, untested car. The reaction of the race organizers can only be imagined. This also proved to be the last race for the W165. It was the year that saw the first and last Yugoslav Grand Prix, held on the same day that Britain declared war on Germany; for the record, Nuvolari won for Auto Union. Grand Prix racing was cancelled for the foreseeable future, even though motor sport continued in Italy and the USA during 1940 and 1941 since both countries remained neutral.

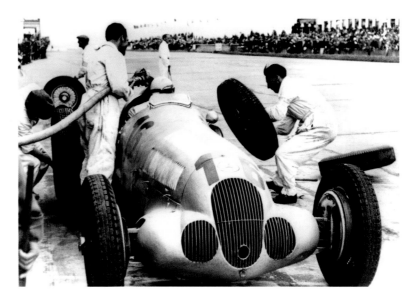

Above: The Mercedes-Benz W154 of Richard Seaman at the 1938 German Grand Prix. The car represented a huge advance in racing technology with its V12 425 horsepower engine and won six Grand Prix races during 1938.

Above: The inaugural Monaco Grand Prix took place on the 14th April 1929. The Mercedes SSK of Rudolf Caracciola was a firm favourite to score a prestigious victory but a brilliant drive in a Bugatti T35B by a British amateur driver, who raced under the title of 'W. Williams', upset the form book. The race around the principality of Monaco was organized by a wealthy cigarette manufacturer and founder of the Automobile Club de Monaco, Anthony Noges, with the approval of Prince Louis II. 'Williams' was Charles Frederick William Grover-Williams, who was a local resident and worked as a chauffeur. His victory at Monaco in his green Bugatti has become part of Grand Prix legend, but he was a driver of some ability since he also won the French Grand Prix in the same year.

Right: During the late 1920s, many large manufacturers left Grand Prix racing due to the restrictions introduced to try to reduce speeds. As a result, the French sporting authority, the ACF, did not receive a single entry for the traditional Grand Prix in 1930. The club organized a Formula Libre race for the July date and promptly set another date in September for another race to be held in Pau. All French manufacturers and drivers were entreated to attend, while conflicting races meant that few foreign teams or drivers could attend. In the end, 37 entries were received, mostly privately entered Bugattis. The race was won by car number 44, the Bugatti T35C of Philippe Etancelin (shown here), a cloth merchant, who drove a steady race to conserve his tyres while all the faster Bugattis had to stop to change tyres on a regular basis. Etancelin won the race from the 4.5-litre Bentley of Tim Birkin.

Above: During 1931, the 'free formula' (Formula Libre) regulations continued, but for a race to qualify as a Grand Prix, it had to last for 10 hours. This necessitated the use of two drivers and was adopted for the French, British and Italian races. During the previous year, 1930, Maserati had enjoyed success with its Tipo 26M, although it proved less competitive in 1931 in spite of the engine producing over 200bhp. The revised Tipo 8C-2800 took third and fourth places at the ACF Grand Prix at Montlhery; the photograph shows the Maserati of Rene Dreyfuss and Pietro Ghersi that finished in eighth place.

Above: The Alfa Romeo 8C-2300 of Tazio Nuvolari leads the Bugatti T51 of his great rival Achille Varzi during the 1933 Grand Prix de Monaco in one of the greatest motoring duels ever witnessed. Varzi set the fastest lap of the 3.14 kilometre circuit in 1 minute 59.0 seconds, but the duel ended on the final lap when the engine of the Alfa expired. Nuvolari attempted to push the car to the finish but collapsed just 200 metres from the line. He was ultimately disqualified when his mechanics tried to help. At the time, the car had to cross the finish line to be classified, but by today's regulations, Nuvolari would have been awarded third place.

Left: Although the 1933 Grand Prix de Nice was not an official World Championship event, it was significant for the appearance of Tazio Nuvolari in a Maserati 8CM. Unhappy with the reliability of the Scuderia Ferrari Alfa Romeos, following the withdrawal of the factory-entered Alfa Corse team, Nuvolari formed his own team with Baconin Borzacchini and Maserati. While Alfa Romeo was in disarray, Nuvolari won the Belgian Grand Prix, the Coppa Ciano and the race in Nice. Shown here at the start, the Alfa Romeo (24) of Philippe Etancelin and the Alfa of Luigi Fagioli (6) led the field away. Etancelin retired and Fagioli finished fourth as the race belonged to the 41-year-old 'Flying

Above: The 1934 season saw the introduction of the 750kg formula that resulted in Grand Prix cars being substantially redesigned. The year also saw the return of Daimler-Benz at the expense of the Italian teams, Alfa Romeo and Maserati. The three Mercedes-Benz W25 team cars all retired during the 1934 French Grand Prix which enabled Alfa Romeo to make the most of the unusual situation and bring its 8C-2900 cars home in the first three places. Louis Chiron (12) won the Grand Prix, with Achille Varzi (6) second and Carlo Trossi (20) third.

Above: The French Grand Prix of 1934 saw the arrival of a new 3.2-litre eight-cylinder version of the Bugatti Type 59. The car proved uncompetitive, expensive to maintain and lacked reliability; it was no longer a match for the new cars from Mercedes and Audi. The supercharged engine produced 240bhp but the cable-operated brakes were a weak point. It used brake drums that were integrated with the wheels so that both had to be replaced at the same time. The Grand Prix saw Tazio Nuvolari at the wheel of a factory-entered Type 59 but both he and Rene Dreyfus retired, while car number 16 of Robert Benoist struggled home in fourth and last place, four laps adrift of three Alfa Romeos.

Above: When Mercedes unveiled its new W25 Grand Prix car in 1934, every other team realized they faced a serious challenge, especially since the Mercedes team leader was the formidable Rudolph Caracciola, seen here at the ACF Grand prix at Montlhery. He was backed up by Manfred von Brauchitsch and Luigi Fagioli. The German team took the French Grand Prix very seriously, sending two cars to practice on the circuit two weeks prior to the race. After official practice, Mercedes, Auto Union and Alfa Romeo were evenly matched and during the first laps of the race, a new average speed of 90mph was recorded. Between laps 10 and 16, all three Mercedes retired with minor problems, but everyone knew they would return and be more reliable than ever.

Opposite: In 1932, Auto Union was created, combining four struggling German manufacturers; Audi, Horch, Wanderer and DKW. It was decided to promote the new company by creating a new Grand Prix car. To save time, a design project was acquired from Ferdinand Porsche and Karl Rabe that continued the mid-engine Benz Tropfenwagen project of 1923, and was built around a new Porsche V16 engine. The Auto Union Grand prix car was a new, low, streamlined design with the driver located close to the front wheels and the fuel tank placed between him and the front of the engine. Hans Stuck qualified the car on the front row of the grid at the 1934 French Grand Prix and ran in the top three places until the car was sidelined with a water leak after 32 laps.

Above: It could be claimed that the 1935 French Grand Prix was not Bugatti's finest hour, nor a great advertisement for the sport. Just one Bugatti Type 59 was entered for Robert Benoist to take on the might of Mercedes, Auto Union, Alfa Romeo and Maserati. To help the situation, the ACF added three new chicanes to the Montlhery circuit to put extra strain on the brakes of the faster cars and allowed a road-going Type 59 to practice for the race. When the Grand Prix car arrived at midnight, it was parked in the Bugatti garage without being scrutineered. It was a very embarrassing moment when the bonnet flew off to reveal a huge 4.9-litre engine that must have taken the car well over the minimum weight limit. However, Benoist demonstrated considerable skill when he caught the bonnet as it parted company with the Bugatti. The car retired on lap 16.

Left: 1936 was the year of the Auto Union Type C since it dominated Grand Prix races. In response, the organizers of the French Grand Prix decided that its race should be run for sports cars. Since Auto Union did not possess a sports car, the plan worked and a French Bugatti won the race, although in reality, France did not host a true Grand Prix that year. Bugatti created the Type 57G, based on its 57S road car chassis, with fully enclosed 'Tank' bodywork, to contest sports car races such as the Le Mans 24-Hours. The record books show that the Type 57G won the 1936 French Grand Prix, driven by Jean-Pierre Wimille and Raymond Sommer.

Opposite: The unofficial World Champion driver for 1936, Bernd Rosemeyer, in action at the Swiss Grand Prix, held in Bremgarten. (The Championship was still contested between manufacturers). Despite Tazio Nuvolari driving his Alfa Romeo as hard as he could, he was unable to match the Auto Unions. One of the most remarkable aspects of the Auto Union Type C was the fact that its designers had installed a 6-litre 520 horsepower engine in a car that met the 750kg weight limit. Rosemeyer won the German and Italian Grand Prix in 1936 and in the Swiss event, he led home Achille Varzi and Hans Stuck to make it an Auto Union 1-2-3. During the race, he had to force his car past the ill-handling Mercedes of Caracciola which caused a difference of opinion that continued long after the race.

Left: The beautiful Vittorio Jano-designed Alfa Romeos of the Alfa Corse team at the start of the 1937 Monaco Grand Prix. Sadly, the best years were behind them as technology progressed and the cars from Mercedes-Benz and Auto Union became faster and more reliable. Not even a new V12 4064cc supercharged engine could redress the balance. The Alfa Romeo (26) of Giuseppe Farina finished in sixth place behind four Mercedes and an Auto Union, while the car of Antonio Brivio (22) retired after 21 laps with radiator problems.

Above: Mercedes-Benz unveiled its W125 Grand Prix car in 1937. Rudolph Caracciola is shown here on his way to winning the Swiss Grand Prix as the team finished in first, second and third places.

Left: The Alfa Romeo Tipo C of Giuseppe Farina being weighed in the scrutineering bay prior to the 1937 Monaco Grand Prix. Farina was the fastest of the Alfa Romeo drivers but even he qualified six seconds slower than the Mercedes-Benz of Caracciola during practice. The first eight places on the grid were occupied by either Auto Union or Mercedes, leaving the five Alfa Romeos and three Maseratis to chase the German cars. Since only two Auto Unions retired, Farinas reward was sixth place, three laps behind the winning Mercedes of Manfred von Brauchitsch.

Opposite: The Mercedes-Benz W154 of Manfred von Brauchitsch at the 1938 German Grand Prix. New regulations for this season allowed engine capacities without superchargers to be set at 4500cc, or 3000cc with a supercharger and a weight between 400kg and 850kg depending on engine capacity. It was hoped that this would allow smaller-capacity cars to compete on equal terms, but in the end, all teams opted for maximum power at the expense of maximum weight. The German Grand Prix was held at the new 22.8 kilometre Nürburgring circuit and von Brauchitsch annexed pole position by six seconds as the W154s occupied the first four grid positions ahead of four Auto Unions. The fastest Alfa Romeo was 43 seconds slower. During a pit stop, fuel ignited and von Brauchitsch was fortunate to escape unharmed. The fire was extinguished and he was able to continue until he crashed at speed and was once again lucky to survive. The race was won by the only British driver in the Mercedes team, Richard 'Dick' Seaman.

Above: The Mercedes-Benz team and the W154 at the 1938 German Grand Prix. From left: Manfred von Brauchitsch, racing manager Alfred Neubauer, Richard Seaman, Hermann Lang and Rudolph Caracciola. Seaman and Caracciola finished first and second, over five minutes ahead the Auto Union cars.

Right: The Mercedes-Benz W154 of Hermann Lang leads the field away at the start of the 1939 ACF Grand Prix at Reims. Due to the unstable political climate in Europe, many races were cancelled and the Italian events were restricted to 1.5-litre voiturette cars. This left the season to be contested between the 3-litre supercharged cars of Mercedes-Benz and the Auto Union Type D that now featured a two-stage supercharger. The Mercedes made the best use of the long straights, reaching speeds of 185mph to take the first three places on the grid. However, this was not to be their day as Caracciola crashed on the first lap and the high speeds created engine problems for the remaining cars. The Auto Union of Nuvolari broke its gearbox, leaving Hermann Muller to record his only Grand Prix victory. Two French Talbots finished in third and fourth places, three laps behind the Auto Unions.

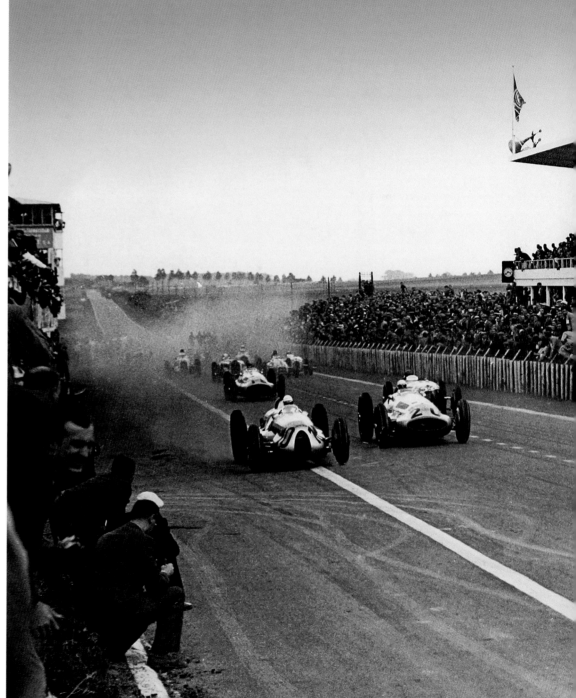

Above: At the Tripoli Grand Prix, May 7th 1939, Hermann Lang brought the 1.5-litre W165 home ahead of his team-mate Caracciola, to record a remarkable victory with a car that was designed and built in just eight months.

Right: Mercedes-Benz created a sensation when it arrived at the 1939 Tripoli Grand Prix with its W165, a miniature 1.5-litre version of the 3-litre W154. The cars finished first and second but never raced again.

3 REBIRTH, THE BRITISH 'GARAGISTAS' AND A RETURN TO POWER

(1946–1969)

Although the Second World War postponed the relentless evolution of racing cars, it also saw an increase in technical research; disc brakes, turbocharging, monocoque construction and fuel injection systems were developed for military use but soon found applications in motor sport. The pre-war Auto Unions had given an indication of future trends, but the cars would not return as the factory had been obliterated by concerted allied bombing; Daimler-Benz faced a similar long process of reconstruction. It would be some time before a German manufacturer could produce anything without seeking permission from the Allied army of occupation.

The war ended in Europe in May 1945 and in September a motor race was held around a makeshift circuit on the Bois de Bologne in Paris. Alfa Romeo and Maserati once again became the dominant marques, particularly the Alfa Romeo 1.5-litre Type 158 voiturettes that had been hidden in a cheese factory when the German army moved into Italy in 1943. In 1946, an unofficial World Championship for Drivers was held at eight venues, mostly road circuits in Italy and France and Raymond Sommer amassed the greatest number of points. The most significant event of the year was the creation of the Federation Internationale de l'Automobile (FIA) that replaced the AIACR and formulated new regulations to apply to the available cars by stipulating a maximum of 4.5 litres or 1.5 litres supercharged. These were initially referred to as 'Formula A' cars, but 'Formula 1' soon became the accepted terminology.

During the summer of 1945, Enzo Ferrari and his chief engineer, Gioachino Colombo, designed a supercharged V12 engine that appeared in the first new car built to Formula 1 regulations, the Ferrari 125. Three cars were entered in the 1948 Italian Grand Prix and the 125 of Raymond Sommer came home in third place. Enzo Ferrari had parted company with Alfa Romeo during 1939 and agreed a four-year 'no competition' clause before he could be released from his contract and race under his own name. Colombo had joined Ferrari from Alfa Romeo, only to return having designed the V12 engine; Aurelio Lampredi took over and created the Tipo 166 sports car. A 166 was entered in the Mille Miglia for Tazio Nuvolari who, despite health problems, had lost little of his skill and determination. In the 1000-kilometre race, he established a 29-minute lead but nearly destroyed his car in the process; even the seat broke away, so he continued by sitting on a box of oranges. During a stop in Maranello, Ferrari saw he was ill and coughing blood, but Nuvolari ignored the pleas to stop and raced on to Parma where he crashed when the Ferrari lost its brakes. Unable to walk, he was carried from the car and nursed back to health by a priest, although he never regained the strength to race again. The era of Nuvolari was over.

At the 1948 French Grand Prix in Reims, a virtually unknown Argentinean driver entered a Simca-Gordini but the car failed to make it to the finish line. Juan Manuel Fangio had been 'discovered' by Jean-Pierre Wimille whilst racing in South America, and he was greatly impressed by what he saw. Fangio had enjoyed success for many years in South America and was awarded a grant by the Argentinean Automobile Club to travel to Europe in 1948 on a fact-finding trip, with a more organized visit planned for 1949, along with a Maserati 4CLT. He was able to enter six regional Grand Prix races in France and won five, finishing second in the unofficial championship, just two points behind Emmanuel de Graffenried, who contested all 11 races. At the time, Fangio was 37 years old but would go on to win five World Championships and become many people's contender for the title of the greatest driver of all time. (Naturally, this remains an impossible title to bestow due to the wide variance in cars, race distances, technology and countless contributing factors; when one considers Fangio's age, innate skill, car control, near-total domination in open-wheel cars, plus his legendary sportsmanship – rarely witnessed today – then he must rate alongside any other contender for the imaginary title).

1948 saw the first British Grand Prix since 1927, held at a disused airfield called Silverstone. Luigi Villloresi and Alberto Ascari finished in first and second places for Maserati. At the end of 1948, Alfa Romeo decided to withdraw for a year despite winning every Grand Prix it entered during the year. Cost was a factor but the death of its most successful driver, Jean-Pierre Wimille, during a race in Argentina, and the loss of Carlo Trossi, due to illness, were also contributing factors. The major races of 1949 were contested by Maserati, Ferrari and Talbot-Lago. Louis Chiron won the French Grand Prix for Talbot, but it was Ferrari that became the most successful team during the year. At the end of 1949, the FIA announced that from 1950, a World Championship for Drivers would be established to give new impetus and interest to the sport, contested by Formula 1 cars. Another major decision that would later have considerable impact in Grand Prix racing was the creation of a new category, Formula 3, for cars using 500cc engines. This acknowledged the growth in popularity of the cars built by British garage owner Charles Cooper, who was developing the mid-engine design that was first used successfully by Auto Union in 1934. (The success of Cooper and others like him led to the British manufacturers being referred to by the Italian teams as 'garagistas', since many built their cars in small lock-up garages.)

The first two years of the new drivers championship saw the Alfa Romeo of Giuseppe Farina winning in 1950 from Fangio, with Luigi Fagioli third despite being nearly crippled by rheumatism at the age of 52. Ascari was fourth, driving a Ferrari. Fagioli was replaced by Felice Bonetto in the Alfa Romeo team while Jose Froilan Gonzalez joined Ascari at Ferrari. The new cars from Maranello showed promise during 1950 when Ascari finished second at Monaco and Monza, but he should have capitalized on Alfa's main weakness – fuel consumption. The 159 could only achieve 1.6mpg and required at least two extra fuel stops despite fitting extra fuel tanks within the engine bay! By the time the Ferraris became competitive in 1951, when Gonzalez finally beat the Alfa Romeos at the British Grand Prix, Fangio had already amassed sufficient points to win his first World Championship. A promising young British driver appeared at the first Grand Prix of the year, in Switzerland, but it would be a further four years before Stirling Moss became a household name.

It was clear that Alfa Romeo would need to re-engineer its supercharged engine to meet the Ferrari challenge for 1952, as the latter's normally-aspirated V12 engines were clearly superior. Eventually, the Ferrari V12 put an end to the use of supercharging in Grand Prix racing. Faced with the prospect of defeat and continuing financial difficulties, Alfa Romeo withdrew. This presented the FIA with a dilemma since they now needed to attract more teams into the sport, so had little option but to put Formula 1 'on hold' as they announced that, for the next two seasons, the drivers championship would be run to Formula 2 rules. This would allow teams sufficient time to prepare Formula 1 cars for 1954 when the engine limit would be 2.5 litres or 750cc supercharged. Formula 2 had been growing in popularity since 1948 and this gave several other teams the opportunity to race against the top drivers, including teams from Britain, France and Germany. Ferrari already had a suitable car, the 2-litre Tipo 500 and Maserati, which had acquired the services of Gioachino Colombo, built the 2-litre A6GCM. The British teams consisted of Cooper, HWM, Frazer Nash and Connaught, while Gordini arrived from France and AFM from Germany, using BMW engines. The drivers and entrants lacked the experience of the Italian teams and they were generally outclassed. Maserati had hoped the services of Fangio would help its cause but, early in the year, he made an uncharacteristic error and broke his neck in a crash. He survived the injury but did not race for the rest of the year. Ferrari dominated the season taking the first four places in the championship as Ascari took the title ahead of Farina and Piero Taruffi.

Juan Manuel Fangio returned in 1953 to drive alongside Gonzalez and his protégé, Onofre Marimon, in Maseratis. The Cooper team lost its best driver when Mike Hawthorn signed for Ferrari. At the start of the season, Ascari was unbeatable, winning his ninth consecutive race at Spa before Fangio could score any points. Fangio won the final race at Monza and, with three second places, finished second in the championship behind Ascari, ahead of Farina and Hawthorn. For 1954, the FIA reverted to Formula 1 regulations and adopted the 2.5-litre engine limit. The most anticipated return was that of Mercedes-Benz which had begun preparing a car for the new formula in 1952 and had enjoyed some success in sports car racing. Lancia also entered the fray when Gianni Lancia took over the company from his father and employed Vittorio Jano to design a suitable car. Alberto Ascari was persuaded to drive for the team but this proved an error of judgement on his part since the car was not ready for the start of the year and technical problems meant he had wasted a year. Fangio won the first two

Above: Juan Manuel Fangio, seen here driving a Mercedes 300SL sports car in 1955, established an indelible reputation in motor sport due to his total mastery in open-wheeled Grand Prix cars, and his quiet determination.

Grand Prix at the wheel of a Maserati 250F, a design that had evolved from the A6GCM, before his Mercedes-Benz W196 was ready to race at the French Grand Prix. He and team-mate Karl Kling lapped the entire field in the new 'Silver Arrows' cars that had fully-enclosed streamlined bodywork that made all other Grand Prix cars look like museum pieces. The dominant Italian teams were left in a sate of confusion as their reign was clearly over. A loophole in the regulations allowed Formula 1 cars to run with enclosed bodywork but this caused problems for the Mercedes drivers at the British Grand Prix, when they had difficulty seeing the apex of the corners; Fangio hit several marker cones to the detriment of the bodywork and Gonzalez took victory in a Ferrari. Mercedes responded immediately by building an open-wheel version of the W196 that proved just as successful, while the streamlined bodywork proved more effective at fast circuits such as Monza.

Stirling Moss began to put in some competitive performances in his Maserati 250F and was leading the Italian Grand Prix until the car failed nine laps from the end, allowing Fangio to record another victory. Mike Hawthorn won the final race in Spain, where the reluctant Lancia D50 finally appeared; Ascari sent out a warning to the Mercedes team by taking pole position and the fastest lap of the race before the clutch failed after ten laps.

The return of Mercedes-Benz caught all other teams off-guard and its cars proved even more effective during 1955 as Fangio and his new team-mate, Stirling Moss, ran away with the championship. Moss had been signed by Mercedes because it had entered the Sports Car World Championship with a car based on the W196, the 300SLR. He proved to be faster than Fangio in sports cars, due in part to his ultimate commitment, while the older, cautious Fangio usually had his measure in open-wheeled cars, thanks to his clinical precision and remarkable strength. The first race of the season was held in blistering heat in Argentina; Moss had to retire due to the conditions, even though he used a reserve driver, while Fangio drove to victory as one of only two drivers to complete the full distance unaided. At Silverstone in 1955, Moss beat Fangio to the line by a matter of inches after racing wheel to wheel and to this day, he still does not know whether the 'maestro' allowed him to win his home Grand Prix.

At the Monaco Grand Prix, Alberto Ascari and his Lancia D50 made a little footnote in history when he drove into the harbour without injury, but just four days later he was killed in a sports car at Monza. Italy was plunged into mourning as its finest driver died and Gianni Lancia decided that the sport held no further interest for him. The D50s had failed to deliver the promised results and he was losing money at an alarming rate. He sold Lancia and handed over his Grand Prix cars, along with the spares, mechanics, drivers and designer Vittorio Jano, along with sponsorship money from the Agnelli family, to a very fortunate Enzo Ferrari, whose own cars had been less than competitive in the face of the Mercedes onslaught.

1955 saw the worst disasters ever witnessed in motor racing and the repercussions would change the face of the sport for ever. At the Le Mans 24-Hours, a Mercedes 300SLR ploughed into a packed spectator enclosure, killing 84 people and the driver, Pierre Levegh. For months, the future of motor sport hung in the balance; Switzerland promptly banned all forms of motor racing on a permanent basis while France only allowed further racing after stringent safety inspections at the tracks. The championship continued and Fangio took the title once more, but Mercedes had to bow to political and shareholder pressure and withdrew at the end of the season. Fangio moved to Ferrari for 1956 and fought off the challenge of Stirling Moss in his Maserati 250F to win once again. British driver Peter Collins took over the Lancia-Ferrari and finished a close third in the championship, while Mike Hawthorn found himself driving for several teams without success. In the final race of the year, Fangio's Ferrari suffered steering failure and in an act of remarkable generosity, championship contender Collins handed over his car to allow Fangio to collect enough points to beat Moss to the title.

In 1957, Fangio had become exasperated by the cars and management at Ferrari and left to rejoin Maserati where he was reunited with one of his favourite cars, the 250F. However, the dominance that the Italian teams enjoyed (excluding the two Mercedes years) was coming to an end as teams from Britain began to take up the challenge. Also, many of the finest post-war drivers such as Froilan Gonzalez, Luigi Villoresi, Giuseppe Farina, Alberto Ascari and Jean-Pierre Wimille, were either dead or retired. To make matters worse, 1957 witnessed another serious incident during the Mille Miglia. The Ferrari of Alfonso de Portago burst a tyre at 170mph and scythed through a group of spectators, slammed into an earth bank and careered along the road. It left both de Portago and his co-driver dead, along with nine people, five of whom were children. It cast a dark shadow over Italian motor sport and the Mille Miglia was never run again.

The year saw the arrival of a new British team, Vanwall, which signed Stirling Moss, Tony Brooks and a highly rated young driver, Stuart Lewis-Evans. A wealthy private entrant, Rob Walker, also joined the Grand Prix events with a modified Formula 2 Cooper-Climax driven by Jack Brabham. By the time of the 1957 British Grand Prix, Fangio had the lead in the championship but by the end of the race, the British Vanwall team had served notice on the Italian teams as Stirling Moss became the first British driver to win a Grand Prix since 1923 and the first British car and driver combination to win the British Grand Prix. The next race, in Germany, did not suit the Vanwall cars since the Nürburgring was notoriously bumpy. Fangio had to win to secure his fifth title, but his car would have to stop to refuel while the Ferraris could carry sufficient fuel to the end. After his pit stop, Fangio drove the Maserati up to and beyond its limits in his pursuit of the three leading Ferraris, breaking the lap record each time as he caught and passed Mike Hawthorn on the final lap, winning by three seconds in what was undoubtedly one of the finest drives ever seen in Formula 1 racing. Hawthorn must have thought the title would be his when he joined Ferrari but the Lancia-Ferraris could not match Fangio and the improving Vanwall of Moss that finished second in the championship. Ferrari failed to win a race but was encouraged by the news that both Fangio and Maserati had decided to retire during 1958.

The new season saw a rule change that banned drivers from swapping cars during a race while all cars had to run on commercially available fuel, so they now made use of aviation fuel. It was not until the sixth Grand Prix of 1958 that Mike Hawthorn gave Ferrari another victory, in France, although a series of second place finishes allowed him to secure the drivers title by one point from Stirling Moss and become the first British World Champion.

Although he had achieved the ultimate prize in the sport, he was devastated by the loss of his friend Peter Collins during the year. He retired to run the family garage business, only to die three months later in a road accident.

1959 proved to be a pivotal year in Formula 1 when the Vanwall team withdrew unexpectedly and a small, rear-engined car took the World Championship in the hands of Jack Brabham. The combination of car and driver were not considered a threat at the start of the season since Brabham had only amassed three championship points during the past four years and the Cooper team were no match for Ferrari. Brabham surprised everybody as he beat the Ferrari of Tony Brooks to the title as Cooper cars claimed five of the top nine places in the championship. At the start of the new decade, Grand Prix racing saw the end of the front-engined cars and a new era began. As expected, a rear-engined car took the 1960 title, with Brabham winning again from the Cooper of Bruce McLaren; Stirling Moss was third in a Lotus 18. Moss's season had been ruined when he broke both legs at Spa, although he returned to win the USA Grand Prix at the Riverside circuit in California.

The FIA changed the regulations for 1961, reducing engine capacity to 1.5 litres. Ferrari already possessed a suitable V6 engine but the British teams of Cooper and BRM argued against the change, with the result they were not prepared for the start of the season. The Ferrari Tipo 156 'shark nose' cars were the most successful that year, with the American driver Phil Hill winning the title from Wolfgang von Trips, who lost his life in the penultimate race at Monza when he collided with the Lotus of Jim Clark. Stirling Moss finished third, having won two races at Monaco and Germany despite the power disadvantage of his Lotus 18. At the French Grand Prix, Giancarlo Baghetti became the first Italian driver to win a Grand Prix since Ascari and the first driver to win on his debut.

The following year, 1962, saw the British BRM team make progress with its V8-engined cars. Bruce McLaren moved to Cooper as Brabham left to form his own team. Graham Hill had struggled for two seasons with BRM but the new P57 showed promise, which was confirmed when Hill won the first race of the year in Holland. Jim Clark responded with the Lotus 25 and the two drivers fought for supremacy throughout the year. The championship was decided at the final race in South Africa, when Clark retired and Hill became World Champion. Ferrari lost the promising young Mexican Ricardo Rodriguez, who died at the age of 20 and the brilliant Stirling Moss had his career cut short following a serious crash at Goodwood. Although he survived, he knew he could not compete at the highest level again, leaving Jim Clark to become the leading driver at a time when a number of talented drivers were competing; John Surtees, Jack Brabham, Bruce McLaren and Graham Hill would have succeeded in any car at any time, but these skilful, competitive racers made an invaluable contribution to a wonderful period in Formula 1, even though too many talented people were lost to the sport.

In 1963, the combination of Jim Clark and Lotus saw the quiet Scottish farmer take seven victories to win the title and establish his reputation as the finest driver of his generation. 1964 saw ex-motorcycle racer John Surtees become the only driver to win a World Championship on both two and four wheels as his Ferrari beat Jim Clark's Lotus to the title by just one point. 1965 was the final year of the 1.5-litre formula and the racing proved as close and competitive as ever. Lotus and Brabham used a new Climax V8 engine and Honda joined the world championship. BRM signed another promising Scottish driver, Jackie Stewart, who rewarded the faith shown in him by winning at Monza. The final race of the year took place in Mexico where Ritchie Ginther gave both Honda and Goodyear tyres their first championship victory, but the title passed once again to Jim Clark, ahead of the BRMs of Graham Hill and Jackie Stewart.

To keep Formula 1 at the pinnacle of motor sport, the cars required more power and this was granted in 1966 with the raising of the engine limit to 3 litres. This created a variety of problems for the teams and the title depended on the team that made the right choice. Lotus was left in limbo as Jaguar-owned Coventry-Climax withdrew and a new Ford-financed engine from Cosworth Engineering was still at the design stage. Lotus struck a deal to use the complex H-16 engine built by BRM, while Ferrari adapted its 3.3-litre sports car engine. Cooper Cars was sold to the company that imported Maserati cars into the UK and they revived the old 1957 V12 Maserati engine

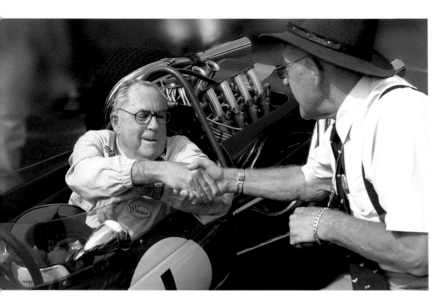

Above: Sir Jack Brabham (in car) and Sir Stirling Moss were among the very best drivers in Formula 1. Seen here at Goodwood in 2004, they have both enjoyed competing in Historic races well into their seventies.

suffering mechanical problems, leaving Clark to win the race, 25 seconds ahead of Jack Brabham. The new engine had proved itself a winner from day one but reliability issues meant that, in spite of winning four races, Clark finished third in the championship, behind the Brabham team cars of Denny Hulme and Jack Brabham, who shared four victories between them.

Jim Clark had won the final two races of 1967 and continued by winning the first race of 1968, in South Africa. This proved to be his final Grand Prix as he lost his life taking part in a Formula 2 race in Germany in April. Colin Chapman and Lotus were devastated by the almost unbelievable loss of such a great driver and a sporting, modest gentleman. It fell to Graham Hill to respond and he did so brilliantly, winning the next Grand Prix in Spain and then at his favourite location, Monaco. Even though reliability remained an issue, he secured the World Championship ahead of the Matra-Ford of Jackie Stewart.

Formula 1 lost four drivers in 1968 as, in addition to Clark, Mike Spence, Ludovico Scarfiotti and Jo Schlesser were lost in various categories of racing. This meant a number of driver changes were made in1969 and Jochen Rindt, who had displayed remarkable skill in Formula 2, was drafted into the Lotus team to partner Hill. However, it was another Scotsman who rose to the top of the sport as the decade came to a close, as Jackie Stewart in his Matra-Ford M80 dominated the 1969 season with six victories from eleven races.

The 1968 and 1969 seasons saw Grand Prix cars dabble in the difficult area of aerodynamics, when the cars acquired high rear (and in some cases, front) aerofoil wings. These devices did little for the car's appearance and controversy arose when both Lotus cars suffered aerofoil failures at the 1969 Spanish Grand Prix. Hill escaped injury but Rindt was fortunate to escape with his life following a huge accident. The governing body, the CSI, were slow to react and when they eventually did take action, it was done in a confrontational manner at the Monaco Grand Prix, The 'wing' design was ultimately a blind alley that came about as designers sought any small improvement in performance to separate the evenly matched cars. At the same time, gas turbine engines and four-wheel drive cars were being considered, without success, as serious research began into aerodynamics.

and Jochen Rindt signed to drive for the team. From the third race of the season, John Surtees joined, having walked away from Ferrari, and with such a strong driving line-up, the Cooper team almost succeeded, but it was Jack Brabham who won the championship. He had commissioned the Australian company, Repco, to adapt an obsolete Chevrolet engine to create a simple but effective 3-litre V8 and a run of four victories secured the title.

The following year saw John Surtees move to the Honda team and Graham Hill joined Clark at Lotus. The most notable occurrence of 1967 was the arrival of the Ford Cosworth DFV engine that was to have a huge impact in Grand Prix racing. It could hardly have had a better introduction when it arrived at the Dutch Grand Prix in the back of the two Lotus 49s, that had been designed to accept the new engine. Graham Hill secured pole position and established a two-second lead during the first lap before

Below: Five races were run to Grand Prix regulations during 1948, one of which was the Albi Grand Prix. The length of race was now reduced although the races lasted for at least two hours and cars were limited to engines of 4.5 litres or 1.5 litres supercharged. In this photograph, Luigi Villoresi powers his Maserati 4CLT around the streets of Albi. The race was run in two heats with Villoresi winning both to secure overall victory from the Talbot T26C of Philippe Etancelin. A relatively unknown car entered the race but retired – a Ferrari 166.

Right: Jean-Pierre Wimille in an Alfa Romeo Alfetta 158 en route to victory in the French Grand Prix at Reims, 18th July 1948. In the absence of the German manufacturers, companies such as Alfa Romeo, Maserati, Talbot Lago and Delahaye took full advantage of the situation even though the absence of Mercedes-Benz and Auto Union diluted the racing. Giocchino Colombo designed the 1.5-litre 158 in 1937 at the request of Enzo Ferrari, with an innovative method of lowering the car's centre of gravity by dropping the location of the rear axle. The Alfa Romeos returned to the track in 1946 and won all 11 races entered during 1948, although the death of Achille Varzi overshadowed the celebrations. It is also worth recalling that a little-known Argentinean driver by the name of Juan Manuel Fangio entered this race in a Simca-Gordini but retired with mechanical problems.

Left: The Talbot-Lago T26C Grand Prix cars enjoyed a successful year during 1949; Louis Rosier is shown driving to fourth place in the French Grand Prix at Reims. Had the official World Championship been instigated in 1949 rather than 1950, Ascari would have won the drivers title while Talbot-Lago would have secured the manufacturers championship ahead of Ferrari. In the absence of Alfa Romeo, the heavy but reliable Talbot-Lago T26C proved an ideal vehicle for many French privateers. Louis Rosier enjoyed considerable success in his Talbot but in this race, Louis Chiron took victory in his similar car.

Above: Peter Walker drives his 4.5-litre BRM Type 15 through the streets of Barcelona in the non-Championship Penya Rhin Grand Prix, 29th October 1950. The British BRM was designed to stem the run of success enjoyed by the Italian marques. The cars of Walker and Reg Parnell showed promise at Goodwood during the year, so they were shipped to Spain to take on the best of the European cars. It proved a fruitless trip as three Ferrari 375s qualified ahead of the two BRMs and both cars retired in the race. Although the British cars were fast, reaching 186mph on the straights, some 8mph faster than the winning Ferrari of Ascari, the Italian cars were quicker by some seven seconds per lap. Spectator protection left a little to be desired.

Above: Alberto Ascari at the wheel of his Ferrari 375 at the French Grand Prix, 1951. An official World Drivers Championship had been established and consisted of eight international Grand Prix including the Indianapolis 500. A further 14 non-championship races were also run to Grand Prix regulations. By now the Ferrari team of Ascari, Froilan Gonzalez and Luigi Villoresi were beginning to threaten the once-invincible Alfa Romeos that enjoyed the advantage of having Fangio in the team. When Ascari's Ferrari failed during the race, he took over the Ferrari of Gonzalez to bring the car home in second place behind Fangio's Alfa Romeo. Such was the dominance of the Italian teams, the three chasing Talbot-Lagos could only come home in seventh and eighth places, six laps in arrears.

Below: The 1951 ACF Grand Prix, held at Reims, was a battle between four Alfa Romeos and three Ferraris. The Alfas of Fangio and Farina were fastest in practice and Farina opened a commanding lead when Fangio's car failed. Fangio then took over the car of Luigi Fagioli while Ascari suffered problems with his Ferrari and took over the car of new team member Froilan Gonzalez. Ascari gave chase but the Alfa of Fangio held on to win. He is seen here taking the chequered flag while Consalvo Sanesi pushes his broken Alfa Romeo across the line, to no avail since he was 19 laps behind Fangio and therefore not classified.

Opposite: The V12 Ferrari 125 of Peter Whitehead in the pits at the Bremgarten circuit during practice for the 1951 Swiss Grand Prix. Behind is the Talbot-Lago T26C of Ecurie Rosier. Whitehead was the first Ferrari privateer owner to take part in Grand Prix racing. He qualified ninth, fractionally slower than Louis Rosier's Talbot but crashed on the sixth lap of the race which took place in pouring rain. The brilliant Fangio took pole position, fastest lap and victory in his Alfa Romeo. Peter Whitehead died in 1958 when his Jaguar slid off a bridge and into a ravine during the Tour de France.

Above: At the end of the 1951 French Grand Prix, Juan Manuel Fangio is almost overwhelmed by admirers in his Alfa Romeo 159. At the time, it was still acceptable for a driver to take over another team member's car if his developed a mechanical problem. When Fangio's car dropped out, Fagioli was ordered to hand his car over and Fangio went on to win. Fagioli had been dropped by the Alfa team at the start of the season but was invited back for this event. However, he was so disgusted at being forced to hand over his car that he retired from motor racing that day.

Opposite: Alfa Romeo mechanics attend the Alfetta 159 of Giuseppe Farina on the grid at the 1951 Spanish Grand Prix. The grid places alternated between Ferrari and Alfa Romeo over the first eight places, followed by three Sunbeam Talbots, five Talbot-Lagos and three Maseratis. Just as he did in the first race of the season in Switzerland, Fangio went on to win the last at the Barcelona circuit, ahead of the Ferrari of Froilan Gonzalez with Farina in third place.

Right: For the 1952 season, Alfa Romeo withdrew from Grand Prix racing since the troubled company lacked the finance to continue the battle against the improving Ferrari team. In an effort to maintain competitive racing without Alfa Romeo, the organizers of the World Championship decreed that for 1952, all Grand Prix would be run to Formula 2 regulations. Ferrari also had experience in this category of racing and, with a driver of Ascari's ability, it swept the board with Ascari winning six of the eight rounds. He even entered the Indianapolis 500 to ensure total dominance, but retired. He is seen here after winning the French Grand Prix at Rouen, the first time the circuit had been used for a World Championship race.

Opposite: Alberto Ascari in his Ferrari 500 en route to victory in the 1953 Swiss Grand Prix. The Ferrari and Maserati cars had a stranglehold on Grand Prix racing during the year, leaving the Cooper, HWM, Oscar and Gordini teams to fight over the minor places. At the Bremgarten circuit, the Maserati of Fangio was on pole, but gearbox problems forced him to take over Bonetto's car. Ascari's Ferrari suffered a misfire which was resolved during a pit stop and, with just 20 laps to run, he rejoined in fourth place behind two Ferraris and a Maserati. When the latter car retired, Ascari had moved into in third place so Enzo Ferrari instructed his drivers to hold position but Ascari decided to ignore him and crossed the line in first place to secure his second World Championship.

Above: Mike Hawthorn (Ferrari 500, left) won the 1953 French Grand Prix from the Maserati A6SSG of Juan Manuel Fangio. This was undoubtedly one the finest displays of Grand Prix driving ever witnessed and thrilled the huge crowd that was privileged to attend that day. For the last half of the race, Hawthorn and Fangio raced side by side or nose to tail, never more than a few feet apart but always giving each other total respect and room on the track in order to avoid contact, since that might spoil the fun. Hawthorn carefully rehearsed his approach to the finish line and his car just had sufficient power to stay ahead of Fangio, the acknowledged maestro. As the unknown Hawthorn stood on the podium with tears in his eyes, the crowd were amazed to see how young he was. It was at this event that Hawthorn established his reputation.

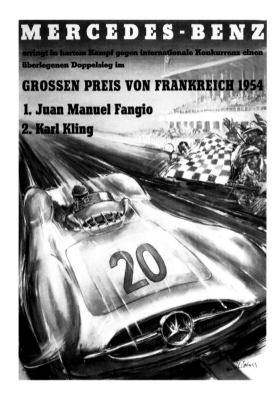

MERCEDES-BENZ

erringt in hartem Kampf gegen internationale Konkurrenz einen überlegenen Doppelsieg im

GROSSEN PREIS VON FRANKREICH 1954

1. Juan Manuel Fangio
2. Karl Kling

Right: During 1954, the German manufacturers made a return to motor sport. Mercedes-Benz prepared a car to comply with the current Grand Prix regulations but it was not ready until the fourth round in France in July. The car that was unveiled was the W196 'Streamliner', a truly magnificent piece of engineering that announced the return of the Silver Arrows. Three team cars were entrusted to Juan Manuel Fangio, Hans Hermann and Karl Kling, Only the Maserati of Ascari (on loan from Lancia) could match the times of the new Mercedes during practice, but his car failed on the first lap of the race. Fangio and Kling ran in convoy to take an uncontested victory while Hermann's car retired with an engine fault.

Above: The 1954 W196 Mercedes-Benz took advantage of a loophole in the regulations to make use of fully enclosed bodywork to gain extra straight-line speed. It used a fuel-injected straight-eight engine of 2496cc that produced 257bhp at 8200rpm. To keep the bonnet line as low as possible, the engine was canted over within the spaceframe chassis. The handling characteristics of the car were never fully resolved, but the inclusion of drivers of the ability of Juan Manuel Fangio and, in 1955, Stirling Moss, in the team meant that average handling was never a serious issue.

Opposite: The Silver Arrows returned to the sport at the French Grand Prix in 1954. Karl Kling (20) and Juan Manuel Fangio (18) power away from the start in the new W196R streamliners. The new Mercedes lapped the field and Fangio crossed the line inches ahead of Karl Kling.

Above: The final Grand Prix of 1954 took place in Barcelona and Fangio drove his Mercedes-Benz W196 to third place. The car shed its enclosed bodywork after the British Grand Prix when the drivers found that the wide body prevented them from placing the car accurately in the corners. The open-wheel bodywork reduced understeer. At the Spanish Grand Prix, Lancia finally unveiled its D50 Grand Prix car in which Ascari secured pole position, with Fangio second alongside the Ferrari of Hawthorn and the Maserati of Harry Schell. The two Lancia D10s retired early and Mike Hawthorn inherited the lead in his Ferrari 553 that he maintained to the end, followed home by Luigi Musso in the fastest of 11 Maseratis. Fangio struggled home in third place, hampered by oil being sprayed back into the cockpit.

Opposite: Due to the blistering heat experienced during the Argentinean Grand Prix, January 16th 1955, an exhausted Stirling Moss was forced to stop before he passed out. His team-mate, Juan Manuel Fangio drove the entire race distance without stopping to record another victory.

Above: The ill-fated Lancia D50 of Alberto Ascari at the Monaco Grand Prix, 1955. This was the first post-war Grand Prix held at the principality and a large entry fought for the 20 places on the grid. Moss and Fangio were given short-wheelbase Mercedes W196s, with Fangio fastest in practice and Moss third, split by the Lancia of Ascari. Fangio made the best start, followed by Castellotti in a Lancia, Moss and Ascari. Moss took second place after five laps but could not close the gap to Fangio. When the axle of Fangio's car broke, Moss inherited the lead until the closing laps when his engine blew. Probably distracted by this event, Ascari misjudged his arrival at the chicane and went straight through the straw bales, into the harbour. Unlike the Lancia, he surfaced and swam to safety, leaving the Ferrari of Maurice Trintignant to take victory.

Above: The Ferrari 555 Supersqualo of Piero Taruffi and the Lancia D50 of Louis Chiron at the Monaco Grand Prix, 1955. Taruffi was drafted into the Ferrari team for this race, where he shared the car with Paul Frere, and the Belgian Grand Prix, although his best years were now behind him. He entered a total of 18 Grand Prix and enjoyed success in sports cars. The veteran Monaco resident Louis Chiron created a record at this event, as the oldest man to take part in a Grand Prix. Born in 1899, he was just weeks away from his 56th birthday and had previously won the Monaco Grand Prix in 1931. He finished in sixth place at this race, five laps behind the winning Ferrari of Trintignant.

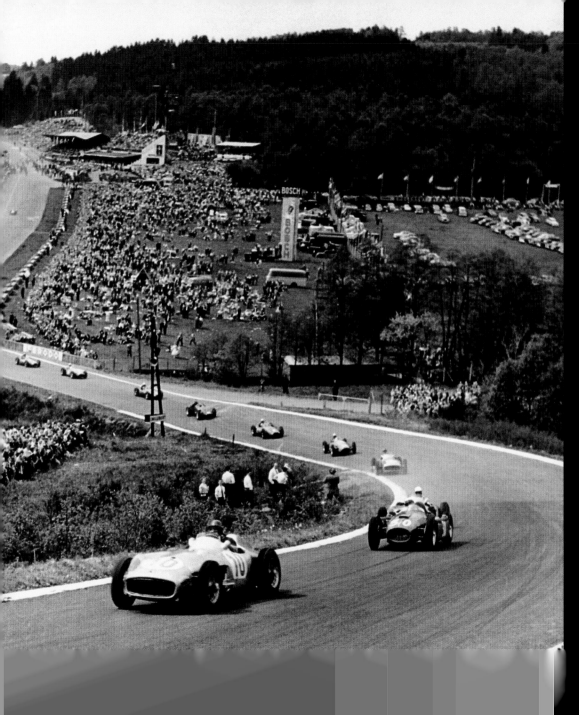

Left: The Mercedes W196s of Fangio and Moss took the first two places at the 1955 Belgian Grand Prix at Spa, running in convoy to the finish. Fangio won four of only seven Grand Prix races that year to secure the drivers title for the second time.

Above: The Mercedes-Benz team arrived at the Italian Grand Prix in Monza knowing that the race would be its last. Following the backlash caused by the Le Mans tragedy, two races had been cancelled and Mercedes-Benz had no option but to close its competition department. A streamlined W196 was entered for Fangio, shown here on the Monza banking, to win the race and another World Championship.

Above: At the 1955 British Grand Prix at Aintree, Moss was pursued relentlessly by Juan Manuel Fangio, both driving Mercedes W196s, all the way to the line. Stirling Moss became the first British driver to win the British Grand Prix, but always suspected that Fangio was the faster driver that day.

Opposite: The BRM P25 of Mike Hawthorn at the British Grand Prix, 1956. The BRM team was established in 1947 by the British Motor Racing Trust, led by Raymond Mays, in an effort to end the Italian domination of the sport. The first car did not appear until 1950 and the team struggled for many years until it won its first race in 1959. In 1956, the new P25 missed the first race, failed to start at Monaco due to engine failure and did not appear at the next three rounds. Three cars were entered for the Silverstone race for Mike Hawthorn, Ron Flockhart and Tony Brooks. Hawthorn qualified on the front row in third place and led the opening laps but between laps 2 and 29, all three BRMs retired.

Opposite: Three Vanwalls were entered in the British Grand Prix of 1956. The cars showed promise in the hands of Harry Schell (16), Froilan Gonzalez and Maurice Trintignant. Gonzalez suffered a broken driveshaft at the start and the other two cars retired with broken fuel lines near the end of the race. The Lancia D50s took the first two places with a fortuitous victory going to Fangio after the leading Maserati 250F of Stirling Moss retired just six laps from the end.

Right: At the 1957 Monaco Grand Prix, the Connaught-Alta B of Stuart Lewis-Evans finished fourth but the race proved to be the final World Championship appearance for the struggling works team and they were not seen again. Connaught had run out of money and the Surrey-based factory closed at the end of the year after seven years of production. Lewis-Evans was a talented driver who earned the respect of his team mates, Stirling Moss and Tony Brooks, when he joined Vanwall in 1958. Sadly his race results did not reflect his ability and he died from burns received in the final race of the 1958 season, following a crash that was caused by mechanical failure.

Above: The Vanwall of Stirling Moss, Monaco, 1957. The Vanwall team was created by Tony Vandervell after he left BRM having decided that the team's committee mentality would prevent it from achieving success. His Vanwalls first appeared in 1954 and Stirling Moss agreed to join the team for the 1957 season. The Monaco Grand Prix saw him qualify in third place and he went into the lead from the start. A rare error resulted in him hitting the chicane on lap 4 which also took out the Lancia-Ferraris of Mike Hawthorn and Peter Collins. Fangio avoided the melee and went on to win in his Maserati 250F, chased all the way by the Vanwall of Tony Brooks.

Below: Peter Collins in the Lancia-Ferrari 801 at the German Grand Prix, 1957. During 1955, Ferrari was struggling and gratefully accepted the ex-Lancia D50 team cars that were given to them when Lancia retired from racing at the end of 1955. The hybrid Ferraris scored several victories in 1956 but during 1957 had a harder time holding off the Vanwalls and Maseratis. At the German Grand Prix, neither Hawthorn nor Collins could hold off the Maserati of Fangio who put on one of the greatest displays of virtuoso driving. The two British drivers were aware that they had been beaten by the better man and carried Fangio shoulder-high along the pit lane. Different times! At the same circuit in 1958, Collins lost his life when his Ferrari 246 spun off the road, throwing him from the cockpit.

Above:. At the German Grand Prix of 1957, the spectators gathered at the Nürburgring were fortunate to witness one of the great displays of driving skill. Fangio, driving an uncompetitive Maserati 250F, opted to run with a light fuel load and refuel after 12 laps, He created a small lead over the faster Ferraris of Hawthorn and Collins before his pit stop. This took 53 seconds and left him 45 seconds in arrears. Fangio held back for another two laps to allow the Ferrari pit to instruct their drivers to ease back since Fangio was not closing. However, with a ten-minute lap time, he could make up a lot of ground before they passed the pits, so he began his pursuit and threw his car around the infamous circuit, breaking the lap record by over eight seconds. By the time the Ferrari drivers realized the danger, it was too late and he took the lead on the final lap to win by 3.6 seconds. It was the final Grand Prix victory for the 46-year old Argentinean and secured his fifth World Championship.

Left: The Ferrari Dino 246 of Mike Hawthorn at the 1958 Monaco Grand Prix. The Ferraris had won two early-season non-championship races, so hopes were high for the Monaco event. However, the British 'garagiste' teams continued to improve and Vanwalls, Coopers and BRMs occupied the first five places on the grid, followed by Hawthorn. By the eighth lap, he had moved his Dino into third place and later inherited the lead as other cars retired. Moss gave chase and passed the Ferrari just before the engine of his Vanwall expired. Hawthorn was back in front, but on lap 46, the fuel pump failed, leaving the Cooper-Climax of Trintignant to win ahead of the Ferraris of Musso and Collins.

Opposite: Maurice Trintignant survived a race of attrition at the 1958 Monaco Grand Prix to bring the Rob Walker-entered Cooper-Climax T45 home in first place, repeating his success at this event in 1955. The Coopers became increasingly competitive when they installed the Climax engine in 1957 and at circuits such as Monaco, the power disadvantage of the 2.5-litre engine was not so critical. The Monaco race was significant as, in 1958, it saw the World Championship debut of Team Lotus and the revival of the Connaught name. Three Connaughts were entered by a car dealer by the name of Bernie Ecclestone, but neither he nor his two drivers could qualify the cars for the race.

Above: At the end of the 1958 season, the Vanwall team withdrew from Grand Prix racing. As a result, Stirling Moss joined the Rob Walker team where he drove a Cooper Climax T51. Seen here at the 1959 Monaco Grand Prix, Moss secured pole position ahead of Jean Behra's Ferrari. Behra took an early lead until Moss found a way past him to lead the Grand Prix until transmission problems caused his retirement on the 81st lap. The gearbox of the Cooper proved to be its weakest link – the works cars used modified Citroën transmissions, but Moss's car used a gearbox built by Colotti which was equally unreliable. Later in the season the Cooper proved more competitive and Moss drove to victory in the Portuguese and Italian Grand Prix to finish third in the championship.

Right: The 1961 season saw the end of the 2.5-litre regulation and the start of a 1.5-litre World Championship. While the British teams argued against the change, Ferrari set about building its beautiful 156 'Sharknose' model, designed by Carlo Chiti, with a 120-degree V6 engine that produced 190bhp. The wide angle of the cylinders allowed the engine to be mounted low in the car to reduce the centre of gravity and the unit was some thirty pounds lighter than the Coventry Climax engine used by the British teams. The photograph shows the 156 of Wolfgang von Trips at the French Grand Prix where he qualified in second place but retired after 18 laps. The race was won by the Ferrari of Giancarlo Baghetti who became the only driver to win a Grand Prix on his debut.

Opposite: The talented American driver, Phil Hill, put his Ferrari 156 on pole position at the 1961 German Grand Prix but that day he had to concede victory to Stirling Moss, who was unbeatable, and his championship rival and team mate, Wolfgang von Trips, who took second place after a long battle, less than one second ahead of Hill. The next race at Monza was to be the showdown between von Trips and Hill to settle the championship but it turned to tragedy when the cars of von Trips and Jim Clark collided. The Ferrari rolled as it ploughed into a spectator enclosure, killing von Trips and 14 spectators. The race continued but when Moss retired, leaving Phil Hill to win the race and the World Championship, there were no celebrations at Monza.

Above: As he did in Monaco, Stirling Moss gave another demonstration of remarkable driving skill to win the 1961 German Grand Prix at the Nürburgring in the Rob Walker-entered Lotus 18. The race was held in damp conditions and when it began to rain near the end of the race, Moss simply extended his lead over the chasing pack. After a long fight, Wolfgang von Trips passed his team mate Phil Hill to secure second place with Jim Clark some way behind in his Lotus 21.

Above: At the first Grand Prix of the 1963 season, held in Monaco, Graham Hill continued as he had finished the previous season, with another victory for BRM. He had secured the World Championship for 1962 at the final Grand Prix in South Africa when his main rival, Jim Clark, had retired his Lotus with mechanical problems. At Monaco, Clark took pole position from Hill and after a slow start, passed Hill and pulled away until his gearbox seized. Hill inherited the lead which he held to the end, followed by his team mate, Ritchie Ginther.

Opposite: The Lotus-Climax 25 of Jim Clark at Monaco, 1963. The Lotus 25 was a revolutionary monocoque design, created by Colin Chapman. The new 1.5-litre formula dictated the need for a small, light car and that was Chapman's forte. Although the monocoque design had been used in the aeronautic industry for over 50 years, Chapman was the first to create a full monocoque chassis. The car was built using box sections, some of which contained the fuel in rubber bag-tanks. The design created a light, rigid car with a much smaller frontal area and a reclined driving position, lying back in the tub. It took a brave driver to adapt to such an unusual driving position, but the car was effective from the start (although Chapman also designed a more conventional spaceframe chassis, the Type 24, just in case). Reliability issues deprived Jim Clark of the title in 1962 and 1963 started in the same manner with another retirement at Monaco. Lotus employed Len Terry to sort the car and from the next race, Clark swept to a record seven victories to secure the World Championship.

Left: BRM introduced a new monocoque design for the 1964 season and Graham Hill gave the P261 an inaugural victory at the Monaco Grand Prix, with the BRM of Ritchie Ginther in second place. The current world champion, Jim Clark, was on pole position in his Lotus but a broken anti-roll bar forced him to stop for repairs. He fought back but was unable to catch Hill prior to the engine breaking near the end of the race. Hill enjoyed a successful season and would have won the World Championship by one point from Surtees had all the points counted. During the 1964 season, only the best six results counted and this allowed Surtees to take the title by just one point.

Opposite: The cars prepare to take their place on the grid at the start of the 1965 Monaco Grand Prix. With Jim Clark busy winning the Indianapolis 500 in America, Graham Hill took pole position and victory in the principality. Alongside him on the front row was the Brabham-Climax of Jack Brabham, followed by Jackie Stewart in a BRM and Lorenzo Bandini in a Ferrari. Tyre technology was improving rapidly and the cars now ran on much wider rubber. 1965 was the final year of the 1.5-litre formula and Jim Clark dominated the season, winning the next five races and the championship.

Above: The BRM P261 of Jackie Stewart at the ACF French Grand Prix, 1967. Thanks to a high rate of attrition amongst the other teams, the uncompetitive BRM finished third behind the two Brabhams, having qualified tenth fastest. In 1967, Graham Hill left BRM and Mike Spence became Jackie Stewart's team mate. The season was not a happy one for the British team since the two drivers could only amass 19 points between them as Stewart retired in nine of the 11 Grand Prix. BRM had intended to use its unnecessarily complex H-16 engine during 1967, but reverted to a more basic V8.

Opposite: At the 1967 French Grand Prix, Dan Gurney attempted unsuccessfully to win his second Grand Prix in his Eagle-Weslake T1G. Just two weeks earlier at Spa, Gurney and Anglo American Racers Ltd became the first American car and driver combination to win a Grand Prix since Jimmy Murphy and Duesenberg succeeded in 1921. Dan Gurney created the All American Racers team in 1964 and designed a car to take part in Indycar and Formula 1 races. To compete in European Grand Prix events, the team established a base in England and commissioned a V12 engine from Weslake Engineering. The engine proved unreliable and the Eagle Formula 1 car took the chequered flag on just two occasions during 1967, winning in France and scoring a third place in Canada. Following an even less successful season in 1968, Dan Gurney returned to the United States to concentrate on Indycar racing.

Below: One of the greatest combinations ever seen in Formula 1 – Jim Clark and the Lotus-Cosworth 49, at the French Grand Prix, 1967. Less than a month before, the pairing had won the Dutch Grand Prix to give the new Cosworth DFV engine a maiden victory. The Ford-financed V8 had been eagerly awaited and the Lotus engineer, Maurice Phillippe, designed the Type 49 to accept it. The combination was quick right from the start and it fell to Graham Hill to establish the first pole position in Holland, but it was Clark who took the victory. The writing was on the wall for the opposition as the Cosworth DFV opened a new chapter in Grand Prix history, going on to win 155 Grand Prix over the next 16 years.

Opposite: 1968 was the year that promised so much but was overshadowed by tragedy. During April, Jim Clark had been scheduled to take part in a sports car race at Brands Hatch but due to some confusion he was sent to take part in an unimportant Formula 2 race in Germany. In pouring rain his car left the unguarded circuit and hit a tree, killing him instantly. He had already won the first Grand Prix of the season in South Africa in January, but by the time of the first European race in May the sport had lost its greatest champion. To compound the problems in the Lotus team, it had also lost Mike Spence who was killed testing a Lotus turbine at Indianapolis. It fell to Graham Hill to help revive Team Lotus and he responded with three victories to win the World Championship. The Type 49B appeared in the colours of a sponsor, Gold Leaf, for the first time in the sport, seen here in the hands of Graham Hill, at the French Grand Prix. He retired with a broken driveshaft while Jackie Oliver crashed the second Lotus in practice.

Opposite: The 1960s were notable for an unacceptably high mortality rate and the 1968 season saw the loss of four drivers prior to the German Grand Prix where this group photograph was taken. The sport lost Jim Clark, Mike Spence and Ludovico Scarfiotti while the popular Frenchman Jo Schlesser died in an underdeveloped Honda in France. From the left, standing and back row: Bruce McLaren, Denny Hulme, Lucien Bianchi, Jacky Ickx, Graham Hill, Chris Amon, Jo Bonnier, Jochen Rindt. Centre row seated: Piers Courage, Jackie Oliver, Jo Siffert, Jackie Stewart. Front row: Kurt Ahrens, Jean-Pierre Beltoise, Richard Attwood, Hubert Hahne.

Right: Matra Sports designed a Formula 3 car in 1965 and by 1968 had entered Formula 1. The French cars were prepared by Ken Tyrrell who signed his friend Jackie Stewart to drive for his team along with Jean-Pierre Beltoise. Matra also designed its own V12 engine although Stewart regularly used a Cosworth DFV. The Grand Prix circus arrived at the Nürburgring in August where it faced the fifth consecutive wet race. Jacky Ickx put his Ferrari on pole by a clear 10 seconds while Stewart (seen here during practice, running without a rear aerofoil) was sixth on the grid. When the flag fell, Stewart moved into third and drove blind in the clouds of spray, fighting his way past Amon and then Graham Hill to ensure he could see at least some of the circuit. In heavy rain and fog he established a 34-second lead by the end of the second lap. To his surprise, the race continued for the full 14 laps in spite of the appalling conditions and he managed to keep control of the car to finish 4 minutes 3 seconds ahead of Graham Hill. Stewart joined the elite rank of driver who had conquered the Nürburgring with a masterful performance. Although Stewart won in Holland and the USA, it was the Lotus that was more consistent and Hill went on to secure the title for 1968.

Left: For 1968 the French Grand Prix returned to Clermont-Ferrand. A number of teams had left Grand Prix racing (Honda, Eagle, Cooper and Matra Sports) and Ferrari entered just one car at most events for Chris Amon. Sadly, it was year to forget due to the near-total dominance of the Cosworth DFV engine. Matra Sport withdrew its V12 engine but Ken Tyrrell continued to run Jackie Stewart and Jean-Pierre Beltoise in Matra chassis using Cosworth power. Seen here en route to victory in the French Grand Prix, Stewart dominated the season and ran away with the championship but the opposition was poor – only 13 cars entered this Grand Prix and the Tyrrell-Matras finished first and second.

Opposite: Jacky Ickx took part in his first Grand Prix in 1967, scoring a championship point in Italy at the wheel of a Cooper-Maserati. Ferrari kept an eye on his progress and signed him at for the start of the 1968 season. He won the French Grand Prix that year but for 1969, contractual problems saw him transfer to the Brabham team in order that he could continue to drive sports cars for the JW Gulf team. At Le Mans in 1969, he won the 24-Hour classic in the closest finish ever witnessed. Seen here in action at the 1969 French Grand Prix, his Brabham-Cosworth BT26A could not live with the pace of Stewart's Matra, although he chased the Matra of Beltoise all the way, but missed taking second place by two-tenths of a second.

4 WEDGES, TURBOS AND SPONSORS

(1970–1989)

The new decade began with several revisions to the cars and their drivers but 1970 belonged to Jochen Rindt and the Lotus 72. The radical new Lotus saw the radiators moved from the front of the car to a position behind the driver where air was fed via large, side-mounted air scoops. This reduced cockpit heat and improved weight distribution, while also permitting a wedge nose, although it left the driver more exposed.

1970 also saw the launch of a much-anticipated new team, March Engineering, with Jo Siffert and Chris Amon as team drivers. March also offered its chassis to other teams, especially Tyrrell, which it realized was facing a dilemma following a split with Matra Sports. Ken Tyrrell was adamant that he wanted to use the Cosworth DFV engine for 1970 in order to remain competitive, while Chrysler-owned Matra could not allow the use of a Ford engine in its cars. No other manufacturer could or would supply a chassis and Stewart refused to drive a Lotus since he was convinced they were built without regard for driver safety. A move to Ferrari was ruled out on the grounds that he would have to part company with Ken Tyrrell (friendship counted for something at the time). In the end, Ford paid for two March chassis and Stewart took the brand new car to a third place in the first Grand Prix and won the second in Spain.

Despite the remarkable start to the year by Jackie Stewart and March, once the Lotus 72 arrived, Jochen Rindt could not be caught and every time the car reached the finish line, it won. Rindt recorded victories at Monaco, Britain, Holland, France and Germany but as he was about to secure a reputation as one of the great drivers in Formula 1, he suffered a fatal crash during practice at Monza. Many drivers, led by a vocal Jackie Stewart, had been arguing that circuits were generally unsafe and should be lined with Armco barriers to prevent cars coming into contact with trees (as with Jim Clark) or spectators. By 1970, most tracks had installed the barriers but not

all were installed correctly and they failed on many occasions. At Monza, the brake shaft broke on Rindt's car and it slammed into the armco, which gave way, the car coming to rest against one of the upright support posts. The whole of the motor racing fraternity was in shock following the loss of the popular Austrian. Lotus withdrew, which allowed the Ferraris of Jacky Ickx and Clay Regazzoni to close the gap on Rindt's championship lead. Lotus decided to return for the final Grand Prix at Watkins Glen, where Emerson Fittipaldi and Reine Wisell finished first and third to ensure Rindt became the first posthumous World Champion.

After his promising start to the year, Stewart's season fizzled out, but for 1971 he had a custom-made Tyrrell 001 at his disposal and this proved very much to his liking, He dominated the season with six victories and was ably supported by a brilliant young French driver, Francois Cevert, who won the final Grand Prix of the year. Stewart had taken over from Jim Clark to become the finest driver of his era. His calculating, analytical approach to racing and natural speed and car control left his rivals struggling in his wake, collecting points wherever they could. He won six Grand Prix during 1971, while no other driver could win more than one.

The early 1970s saw tyres become wider as technology developed and eventually treadless 'slick' tyres became the accepted dry-weather choice; wet weather tyres still required treads to disperse water. The Cosworth DFV engine allowed numerous small teams to enter the sport and gave them the opportunity to compete on equal terms, forcing them to resort to technology, or some subtle gamesmanship, to eke out an advantage. Cosworth did not have things all its own way since the Ferrari V12 engine remained a force to be reckoned with, winning the constructors championship in 1976, 1977 and 1979. Advertising had been banned on cars until 1968 when commercial pressures forced the hand of the rule makers and the doors were opened to allow many people within the sport to become wealthy. It was the small team of Frank Williams, having first entered in 1970 with a chassis from the Italian company, de Tomaso, that fought hardest to eventually win the World Championship and become one of the 10 major Grand Prix teams by the end of the century, thanks in no small part to the sheer bloody-minded determination of its founder. Lotus lost its focus for a while following the loss of Jochen Rindt, although the young Emerson Fittipaldi, who replaced him, was a driver of considerable ability. He went on to prove his worth as he fought with Jackie Stewart to win the title in 1972 to become the youngest World Champion, a record he held until 2005.

Safety remained an important issue in 1973 and the minimum weight limit was raised from 550kg to 575kg to allow for the addition of deformable structures to help protect the drivers. The starting grid layout was changed to two cars per row, a policy which remains to this day. The Swedish driver, Ronnie Peterson joined Emerson Fittipaldi at Lotus where the red and gold livery of the Lotus 72s made way for the distinctive black and gold colour scheme of a new sponsor, JPS. The Ferrari team went into one of its periodic declines, the two cars amassing just 12 points during the season as the Cosworth teams came out on top, while the established British team, BRM, went into terminal decline. The new Tyrrell 006 proved a match for the Lotus 72 and the two teams battled hard throughout the year, with all four drivers capable of winning races. What should have been a classic season was once again plunged into mourning at the final race at Watkins Glen where the young Tyrrell driver, Francois Cevert, lost his life during a practice session. Jackie Stewart declined to take the start of his 100th grand Prix and flew home to a well-deserved retirement, having secured the World Championship once again.

Following the loss of its two top-level drivers, the Tyrrell team regrouped and signed another promising young driver, Jody Scheckter, plus the reliable Patrick Depailler. However, the team would never reach the same heights, although it would be many years before Ken Tyrrell would give up the struggle. 1974 saw Emerson Fittipaldi lose patience with the lack of progress at Lotus and move to McLaren where the M23 proved to be the best Grand Prix car of the time. Ferrari began the slow process of revival, Scheckter gave Tyrrell two Grand Prix victories but it was Fittipaldi who won the title once again. The following year, 1975, a very under-rated driver, Niki Lauda, began to perform wonders in a Ferrari and took the title from Fittipaldi. It seemed certain that he would repeat the performance in 1976 before a huge accident at the Nürburgring left him badly burned and close to death. In one of the most amazing recoveries ever witnessed, and with incredible self-belief, Lauda returned to racing in just six weeks. Had it not poured with rain at the final race in Japan, few doubted that Lauda would have made history, but he had trouble with his vision in the terrible conditions, so took the brave and sensible decision to retire from the race. His rival, James Hunt, hung on in his McLaren to win the championship by a single point.

Two major advances in Grand Prix technology arrived in 1977; Lotus introduced the Type 78 'wing' car that moved the development of aerodynamics forward one step, and Renault returned to top-level motor sport with a car designed to the '1.5-litre turbocharged' rule, which had been overlooked for many years. The 1977 championship was not a classic since the title was won on behalf of Ferrari thanks to the remarkable skill of Niki Lauda. He endured a miserable season due to the faceless troublemakers who used to blight the Ferrari team. They were not impressed by his decision to retire from the 1976 Japanese Grand Prix (he was obviously considered expendable) and began a campaign of undermining their driver's confidence. In response, Lauda hauled the very ordinary 312T2 to another title and, having delivered the goods, left Maranello with two races left in the season. His place was taken by Gilles Villeneuve.

Ferrari's loss was Brabham's gain in 1978 as Niki Lauda joined the team. Colin Chapman designed a remarkable 'wing-car', the Lotus 79 that, in the hands of Mario Andretti and Ronnie Peterson, swept the opposition aside. The wedge-shaped car used side-skirts to channel air beneath the body and create a low pressure area that helped suck the car to the ground in corners. Rather than follow Chapman's lead, Brabham designer Gordon Murray took a different approach and designed a 'fan car' that Lauda took to a maiden victory in Sweden. The result was immediately protested since the huge fan mounted at the rear of the car literally swept the track clean and threw the dirt and gravel into the faces of the following drivers. The victory was allowed, but the fan car was subsequently banned.

Lotus tried to develop its Type 79 even further for 1979 since its replacement, the 80, proved far too complex. In a complete reversal of fortune, the team failed to win a single point. Early in the year, the French Ligier cars took the race wins before Gilles Villeneuve began to get to grips with his Ferrari. Jody Scheckter joined the team and, thanks to better reliability, took the title ahead of Villeneuve, who continued to entertain with his sideways style of driving and incredible commitment. The Williams cars also won races before everyone was granted a glimpse of the future when a Renault, the first turbocharged Grand Prix car since 1907, won the French Grand Prix. By 1980, the 1.5-litre engines were producing about 520bhp but, just five years later, BMW engines gave 1300bhp. New technology and computers allowed engines to be managed by electronics as microchips governed exact ignition timing and fuel delivery. In addition, cars were now built from new lightweight materials such as carbonfibre that was sourced from the aerospace industry. Grand Prix cars were becoming increasingly complex and expensive and, as costs soared, private teams struggled as sponsorship became ever more critical. Naturally sponsors demanded success, so Grand Prix racing moved away from being a sport, enjoyed by gentleman drivers, to become a corporate business with little time for sentiment – the television armchair audience became a new priority.

Even though the FIA demanded the removal of the potentially dangerous aerodynamic side-skirts for 1980, the teams called its bluff and refused to remove them due to the amount of money invested in the cars, which were undriveable without them. During this period, the racing was overshadowed by political arguments between the governing body and the teams' representative committee, which did little to promote the sport. The small teams faced an uncertain future since none possessed the funds to build its own turbo engine, leaving the door open for the large manufacturers such as Renault, Alfa Romeo, BMW and Ferrari to enjoy a substantial power advantage. In 1980, many Formula 1 teams struggled to survive and McLaren were forced to join forces with the Project 4 team headed by Ron Dennis, resulting in the creation of McLaren International. Ferrari suffered a year to forget as its long-suffering drivers, Scheckter and Villeneuve, struggled to amass just eight championship points between them, as the red cars from Maranello retired with monotonous regularity. It was Alan Jones in a Williams FW07 who took the title.

In 1981, the in-fighting between the Federation Internationale du Sport (FISA) that had been created by the FIA in 1979 to control all World motor sport championships, and the Formula One Constructors Association (FOCA) that represented the teams, reached a serious impasse. A form of political stability was eventually established with the creation of the 'Concorde Agreement' that recognized the right of FISA to establish the rules within the sport whilst FISA recognized the rights of FOCA to negotiate the financial deals, plus television rights, subject to the approval of FISA. The agreement arrived too late to save the first Grand Prix of the season although, when peace was established, it was Nelson Piquet in an unusually fast Brabham who took the drivers championship, ahead of the Williams of Alan Jones and Carlos Reutemann. Renault, with Alain Prost in its team, showed greater promise but Ferrari was still on a downward spiral.

No doubt Ferrari thought matters would improve with the introduction of its first turbo car in 1982, but the 126C2 proved to be a failure. Although the car had more power, its chassis left much to be desired. Skirts were now banned and the only way to keep the cars running as low to the ground as possible was to make the suspension harder. This created its own dangers since, if the air beneath the car escaped, downforce was lost and the car generally flew off the track. The cars went round corners as if they were on rails and the huge g-forces generated caused serious problems for the drivers who were also being shaken and battered by the rock-hard suspension. This was not a good time to be a Grand Prix driver.

1982 would be remembered for the loss of Gilles Villeneuve, who had become hugely popular with spectators and fans of the sport. Gilles did not race purely for the world championship, like the majority of drivers; he raced because he loved it and was only concerned about winning each race he entered. He was joined at Ferrari by Didier Pironi and the two drivers agreed that, if they were running together near the end of a race, they would maintain their positions and not risk a collision. Villeneuve was therefore amazed when Pironi forced his way past on the final lap of the San Marino Grand Prix to take the win. Two weeks later, Pironi had set the fastest time in practice in Belgium and Villeneuve, still upset by a perceived act of betrayal, went out to beat the time. He crested a rise only to come across another car that was slowing. His Ferrari slammed into it and took off, killing Villeneuve on impact. It was taken for granted that Gilles Villeneuve would have eventually become a worthy World Champion. Didier Pironi suffered a career-ending accident later in the season but finished second in the championship behind the Williams FW08 of Keke Rosberg. The tragic season saw the loss of Colin Chapman who had guided Lotus to the pinnacle of the sport on seven occasions; without him, Lotus would never again be a force in Grand Prix racing.

In 1983, Brabham acquired a turbo engine from BMW and Nelson Piquet made the best use of it to take the title, ahead of the Renault of Alain Prost and the Ferrari of Rene Arnoux. The engineers within Cosworth could not extract sufficient power from its venerable DFV, although, with its smooth and responsive power delivery, it still proved effective on street circuits. Rosberg threw his Williams around Monaco to win and Michele Alboreto took an unexpected victory for Tyrrell around the streets of Detroit to register the last of 155 Grand Prix victories for the Cosworth DFV.

Williams installed Honda turbo engines from 1984 as every team other than Tyrrell moved to turbo power. It was McLaren with its TAG-Porsche engines that produced the most effective car for 1984, and with Niki Lauda and Alain Prost in the team, the outcome was inevitable. The championship went down to the wire as the two drivers fought throughout the year (without any animosity) but eventually the experience and downright cunning of Lauda won the day as he took the title by only half a point.

The following year, 1985, saw the rise of two other drivers who, along with Prost and Piquet, would dominate Formula 1 for the next eight years; Ayrton Senna and Nigel Mansell. The latter had been unhappy at Lotus

following the death of Colin Chapman and had never delivered in terms of results. His move to Williams, with whom he won his first Grand Prix, allowed him to regain his confidence and finally demonstrate he could be a fast as anyone in the sport. Senna moved to the vacant seat at Lotus and delivered the Grand Prix victories that Mansell did not provide, even though the Lotus was generally out-classed. By now the Grand Prix season had expanded to accommodate 16 races as the television coverage improved and the global audience became of prime concern to the sponsors. With restrictions on tobacco advertising in the media, and a threat of even stronger future sanctions, Formula 1 became increasingly important to the tobacco industry as a means of reaching its target audience. With five race wins during 1985, Alain Prost in a McLaren MP4/2B won the championship comfortably ahead of the Ferrari of Michele Alboreto.

The McLaren MP4, designed by John Barnard, was a highly efficient race car and the TAG-Porsche engine was a remarkable feat of engineering since its 1500cc V6 engine produced 750bhp at 12,000rpm. The revolutions produced by Grand Prix engines were now a long way from the Renault that won the first Grand Prix in 1906, which produced 90 horsepower at 1200rpm. However, it took a mighty engine to create such power, some 8.6 times larger than the TAG-Porsche at 12,986cc. Although 12,000rpm was considered remarkable in 1986, in less than 20 years, larger 3-litre engines would be capable of reaching 18,000rpm without being reduced to component parts. In 1986, Prost once again won the title for McLaren but was chased all the way by Nigel Mansell. It seemed that, with just five Grand Prix left, Mansell had the championship in his pocket. Although Prost closed the gap slightly, Mansell required just three points from the final race in Australia to become the champion, even if Prost won. However, a tyre exploded on the Williams at full speed on the main straight to put Mansell out as Prost was leading. All was not well with the McLaren as the fuel read-out was informing Prost that he did not have enough fuel to reach the chequered flag, and Piquet was closing in. He had to win the take the title, so took a gamble that the fuel reading was wrong and maintained his pace to the end. He was right and the computer was wrong.

Turbo engines were beginning to create problems within Formula 1; not all the drivers liked the on-off power delivery and, as speeds now topped 200mph, they were difficult and dangerous to drive. In practice sessions, special 1300 horsepower engines that had a lifespan of just a few laps merely served to drive costs through the roof. It was decided that, for 1987, the turbo engines would use pop-off valves that controlled fuel-flow and 3.5-litre atmospheric engines in lighter chassis would be permitted. For 1988, further turbo restrictions would apply and, in 1989, they would be banned. It was the combination of Ayrton Senna and the complex Lotus-Honda 99T (using active suspension and, eventually, a semi-automatic gearbox, traction control and anti-lock brakes) that everyone expected to secure the title in 1987, but the Williams-Honda proved to be more effective as Mansell and Piquet won nine of the 16 races.

There were no team orders at Williams leaving the drivers free to race one another. When Mansell went past Piquet in both France and Britain to win in dramatic fashion, Piquet was not amused and decided to move to another team for 1988. Mansell won six races to Piquet's three, while the Brazilian driver had recorded seven second places while Mansell had none. At the penultimate race of the season, Mansell crashed heavily in practice and his season ended, still twelve points behind Piquet. However, Piquet's search for another team took him to Lotus and the reshuffle caused Honda to move its engines to McLaren to accompany Senna. As a result of the move, the McLaren-Honda partnership secured the championship for the next six years.

The combination of Senna, Prost and the McLaren-Honda MP4/4 crushed the opposition throughout 1988. Only Gerhard Berger won for Ferrari at Monza, after Senna was hit by a back-marker. Prost accumulated the largest points total but as he could only count the best 11 results (he never finished lower than second), he discarded 18 points while Senna dropped just four. Thus it was Senna who won the championship by just three points. In August that year, motor racing said farewell to Enzo Ferrari who passed away that month, having overseen his team since the introduction of the World Championship in 1950.

From 1989, all cars ran with a normal 3.5-litre engine and several teams opted for the revived Cosworth DFZ. Lamborghini entered Formula 1 with its V12 engine mounted in a Lola chassis, with little success, while Honda supplied a V10 engine to McLaren. Thus the status quo was maintained as Prost took the title from Ayrton Senna. At first, it seemed as though the other teams might stand a chance as Mansell, now with Ferrari, won the first Grand Prix of 1989, before Senna took charge, winning the next three and Prost responded with a further three. Unfortunately Prost and Senna had totally different philosophies regarding what constituted 'sportsmanship'. Ayrton Senna was committed to winning every race at any cost while Prost accepted that, on occasion, he could be beaten by a better driver. Nobody doubted that Senna was the fastest driver of the time but Prost could, and occasionally did, find the necessary turn of speed to beat Senna in a straight fight, which Senna had a problem accepting and did little to cement any friendship. Prost had tried to establish an agreement that the two drivers would not contest the start of a Grand Prix, thereby avoiding an unnecessary accident. He soon discovered that any 'gentleman's agreement' would prove worthless and matters boiled over at the penultimate race of 1989 in Japan, where the two cars became entangled. Senna had to get past Prost to ensure he won the title, so he placed his car alongside Prost in the chicane, assuming he would naturally give way in order to avoid an accident. For once, Prost decided to turn into the corner and the cars collided; as Prost left his stalled car, Senna called for the marshals to push him clear. When they did, he jump-started the engine and went on to win the race, only to be excluded for missing the chicane. This handed the title to Prost. Senna was appalled and when he refused to stop his protests to the FIA and the press, he was fined and given a suspended ban. Although the Prost-Senna battle made for some lurid headlines and committed action on the track, it did little to convince the general public that Formula 1 had many sporting credentials.

Formula 1 was enjoying a resurgence in 1989 with 20 teams and 40 cars trying to qualify at every Grand Prix, using engines from seven different manufacturers. However, the top four teams gathered 316 points while the remaining 16 shared only 66 points.

Left: John Young Stewart came to prominence when he dominated Formula 3 during 1964 and joined BRM in 1965. He took the first of three World Championships in 1969 to become one of the most famous and recognizable sportsmen in the world, with his distinctive long hair, Beatles cap and Rolex watches. By 1970, he could no longer walk through the paddock without being besieged by autograph hunters, as here at Brands Hatch, March 1970, where he won the Race of Champions Formula 1 event from Jochen Rindt. 1970 was not a successful season in Grand Prix races but in both 1971 and 1973 he secured the drivers title before leaving the sport at the peak of his form.

Opposite: 1970 was the year that the Austrian driver Jochen Rindt finally received the car that complimented his great skill. Shown here at the French Grand Prix, he had already won at Monaco with an old Lotus 49, but when the remarkable Lotus 72 became available he went on to win in Holland, France, Britain and Germany. Engine problems caused his retirement in Austria, but he was a firm favourite to win the Italian race at Monza. Tragically, when he hit the brakes at speed during practice, the Lotus turned sharp left and slammed into the guardrails. The whole motor racing community was in shock as the enormously popular Rindt became the only driver to become a posthumous World Champion.

Right: The Brabham team had great hopes for its BT34 in 1971 but it proved uncompetitive and failed to improve throughout the season. At the end of 1970, Jack Brabham had decided to sell his team and fellow Australian Ron Tauranac (to the right of the picture) purchased a 50 per cent share, while signing Graham Hill to drive for the team for 1971. Hill, standing behind the car, looks perplexed by the BT34 (usually referred to as the 'lobster claw') and nobody else seems any wiser. The car only collected one points finish throughout the season and by 1972 the team had been sold to Bernie Ecclestone.

Above: During 1972, Matra Sports wound down its involvement in Formula 1 and ran only one car for Chris Amon, prior to leaving at the end of the year to concentrate on sports car racing. Amon seemed to attract more than his share of misfortune during his decade in Grand Prix racing. Although he won non-championship Formula 1 races, the Le Mans 24-Hours and many other top class sports car races, he was unable to win a Grand Prix. The French Grand Prix of 1972 (shown here) is a case in point where he qualified on pole but suffered a puncture from the many small stones that littered the Clermont-Ferrand circuit and finished third, 32 seconds behind Stewart's winning Tyrrell 003.

Right: The Lotus-Cosworth 72D of Emerson Fittipaldi won the Race of Champions and the British Grand Prix at Brands Hatch in 1972. Fittipaldi won this and four other Grand Prix to secure the World Championship for that year. He had been elected as number one driver for Team Lotus following the tragic death of Jochen Rindt at the end of 1970. The young Brazilian found results hard to come by during 1971 but his smooth, delicate style of driving and tactical skills came to the fore during the following season, with the new Lotus 72D now painted in the black and gold livery of 'John Player Special'. Although the new car delivered the title to Lotus and Fittipaldi, three other drivers raced the second 72D throughout the year but failed to register a single point between them.

Below: One of the most admired and respected drivers of his generation, 'Super Swede' Ronnie Peterson was destined to become a World Champion until a freak start-line accident robbed the sport of his precocious talent in 1978. (In fairness, Peterson was an intuitive, rather than technical driver; he just drove whatever was given to him up to and beyond the car's capabilities.) He began his career with the March team – shown here taking his March 721 to the Brands Hatch scrutineering bay – but the cars were not competitive, despite Ronnie's best efforts and fearless, sideways driving style. After three frustrating years, he joined Lotus in 1973 and towards the end of the season scored four victories with the 72D to finish third in the championship behind Stewart and Fittipaldi.

Right: The 1973 season saw the Lotus and Tyrrell teams fight it out for the World Championship with McLaren chasing hard to pick up victories when the others slipped. The JPS-sponsored Lotus 72Ds, seen here in the paddock at Zolder in Belgium, were handled by two of the fastest drivers in Formula 1, Emerson Fittipaldi and Ronnie Peterson. The drivers finished second and third in the championship with three and four victories respectively but reliability was not as good as the Tyrrell cars.

Above: Graham Hill at the Belgian Grand Prix, 1973, in the first car to race in the colours of the Embassy-Hill team. This was formed by Hill at the start of the year and the car was built around components from a Shadow with a Cosworth DFV engine. Graham Hill, who had come late to motor sport, became a national hero thanks to his irrepressible sense of humour and two World Championships. He was also the only driver to win the Triple

Below and right. During the 1960s and 1970s, an unacceptable number of talented drivers gave their lives to the sport they loved. Few losses were felt more deeply than that of the hugely talented and popular Frenchman, Francois Cevert. Seen here in the cockpit of his Tyrrell-Cosworth 006 in Belgium and in action at the French Grand Prix, 1973, he finished second in both races, backing up his team leader Jackie Stewart en route to his World Championship. Stewart had realized that, at times, Cevert was faster than him and had decided to retire at the end of the season at the end of his 100th Grand Prix. His plans were left in tatters when Cevert was killed whilst practicing for the final race of 1973, at Watkins Glen, USA. Stewart was grief-stricken at the loss of his friend and walked away from competitive driving on the spot, having won the championship and taken part in 99 races.

Opposite: The Tyrrell 007 of Jody Scheckter, France 1974. Shaken by the tragic loss of Francois Cevert and the retirement of Jackie Stewart, Ken Tyrrell had to regroup. He signed the young hot-shoe driver from South Africa, Jody Scheckter, and another French driver, Patrick Depailler. Scheckter was undoubtedly fast but was still learning the sport while Depailler had a deserved reputation for sheer determination. Scheckter proved his ability by winning in Sweden and Britain, plus a pair of second and third places, to finish third in the championship, whilst Depailler was less successful. He best result was to finish second behind Scheckter in Sweden.

Right: 1974 saw Emerson Fittipaldi win the World Championship in a Cosworth-powered McLaren M23. It was a competitive season in Formula 1 with race victories shared amongst the top seven drivers, as McLaren, Ferrari, Lotus, Tyrrell and Brabham cars took the victories. Fittipaldi took the title by just two points from Clay Regazzoni's Ferrari. During 1974 the McLaren team was divided into two as Teddy Mayer took charge of the Marlboro-Texaco sponsored cars of Fittipaldi and Denny Hulme while Phil Kerr began the season with Mike Hailwood driving a Yardley-McLaren. In 1974, three new teams (Hesketh, Parnelli and Penske) joined the Grand Prix circuit, bringing the number of teams to 18.

Below: Niki Lauda en route to victory in the French Grand Prix, 1975. After 11 years in disarray, Ferrari returned to the top of the Grand Prix results as Lauda took five wins and the World Championship in the new Ferrari 312T, with a new transverse gearbox. Lauda would become a triple world champion and one of the most capable drivers ever to sit in a Grand Prix car. However, his early years showed little promise and when he bought a drive in a March during 1971, he was dismissed as another rich no-hoper. By 1974, he was winning races for Ferrari and took over the role as the top driver in the sport following Stewart's retirement. Only a major accident deprived him of a fourth title. He also set a new precedent when he retired in 1979, created a new airline, returned to Grand Prix racing in 1982 and secured another title in 1984.

Right: James Hunt drives his Hesketh-Cosworth 308 to a strong second place at the 1975 French Grand Prix, having won the previous race in Holland. One of the most unlikely teams to have competed in Formula 1, Hesketh set out to prove that you could still win races whilst having fun. Ex-Formula 3 driver James Hunt was the perfect choice of pilot having been sacked from F3 due to his propensity for throwing his car into the scenery. The team entered Formula 1 in 1974 with a car built in the stable block of Lord Hesketh's stately home. All this jollity was funded by Hesketh's inheritance since sponsorship was considered vulgar. Naturally it could not last, but they proved a point and the breath of fresh air disappeared when they departed from the sport at the end of 1975.

Below: After the Hesketh team ran out of money and Emerson Fittipaldi left McLaren to drive for his brother's Copersucar team, Hunt jumped at the chance to take his place. His earlier reputation for wild driving had been modified by his success with Hesketh and he repaid McLaren with six race victories to take the 1976 championship title by a single point from Niki Lauda in a dramatic final race in Japan. Lauda had just survived a huge accident at the Nürburgring and only six weeks after being given the last rites, returned to the tracks to defend his championship lead. Due to torrential rain during the Japanese Grand Prix, Lauda took a courageous decision to retire rather than risk another accident and Hunt managed to secure the third place he required for the title. Hunt is seen here at the Spanish Grand Prix in 1976, where his car was excluded after the race for being a fraction too wide. Fortunately for his championship hopes, his third place was re-instated following an appeal.

Right: One of the most radical Grand Prix cars of the 1970s was the Tyrrell P34. Instead of the usual two front wheels it used four small 10-inch wheels that designer Derek Gardner hoped would minimize drag by reducing lift and help the car turn into corners more efficiently. 'Project 34' created considerable controversy when it was unveiled at the 1976 Spanish Grand Prix but just two races later, at Monaco, the Tyrrells of Scheckter and Depailler finished second and third. At the next race in Sweden, the cars took first and second, finishing in third and fourth places in the championship. The P34 was withdrawn at the end of the following season due to the problems developing suitable tyres and the ruling body took the opportunity to ban any further six-wheel vehicles.

Below: Niki Lauda with the Ferrari 312T2 at the French Grand Prix, 1977. During the '77 season, Lauda had Carlos Reutemann as his team-mate, who had been brought into the Ferrari team after Lauda's accident in 1976. Despite his injuries, Lauda was determined to prove he was as capable as ever and scored three victories on the way to his second World Championship. In France he could only finish fifth, behind Mario Andretti's improving Lotus 78, which was coming to terms with the science of ground-effects. The 1977 season also saw the introduction of a Grand Prix car that conformed with the alternative choice of engine – 1.5-litre turbocharged, instead of the usual 3-litre normally aspirated. It would take the Renault team a few years to develop the technology but the turbo-car would eventually change the face of Grand Prix racing.

Above: The start of the German Grand Prix at the Nürburgring, August 1st, 1976. From the left, the Ligier (26) of Jacques Lafitte, the Ferrari 312T2 of Niki Lauda (1), the Tyrrell P34 of Patrick Depailler, pole position McLaren of James Hunt and the Ferrari of Gianclaudio 'Clay' Regazzoni. The drivers were concerned about the safety arrangements at the 14-mile circuit but eventually agreed to race. During the first lap, Lauda lost control of his Ferrari on the damp circuit and spun through the catch fencing into an earth bank. The Ferrari was hit by two other cars and following drivers stopped to help pull him from his blazing car. Seriously burnt, he fought for life over the following days and, despite his dreadful injuries, returned to the cockpit just six weeks later.

Above: Jody Scheckter, who joined the Wolf team in 1977, in the process of scoring one of his three victories at Monaco. Walter Wolf made his fortune in North Sea oil and purchased a majority share-holding in Frank Williams's team. During 1976, the revised ex-Hesketh cars that Wolf acquired did not prove competitive so for 1977, the team was restructured. The new Wolf WR1 was designed by Harvey Postlethwaite and Scheckter was lured away from Tyrrell. The Formula 1 world was taken by surprise when the Wolf won the first race of the season in Argentina, followed by further victories in Canada and Monaco. Scheckter went on to finish in second place behind Lauda in the championship.

Left and below: The combination of Mario Andretti and the Lotus 79 proved virtually invincible during 1978. Andretti is shown here in action at the French Grand Prix and in the cockpit of the car in Belgium, where he first drove the 79. Although the new Type 79 was not ready for the start of the season, the previous Type 78 car still proved capable of winning, but when the new car was ready, Andretti made full use of it to secure five of his six victories that gave him the title. The Type 79 was one of the most important and influential Grand Prix cars ever created, since it made full use of aerodynamic ground-effect forces that channelled air beneath the car, greatly increasing downforce that in turn allowed the use of a smaller rear wing, which decreased drag. It is also considered one the most elegant open-wheeled cars ever created and it won on its debut at the Belgian Grand Prix, which also happened to be Colin Chapman's 50th birthday. Although the Lotus team faced strong opposition during 1978, the Lotus 79 was in a different league, as Mario Andretti and Ronnie Peterson proceeded to demonstrate.

Above: Jody Scheckter joined Ferrari for 1979 and confounded the experts by becoming a well-respected member of the team. He is shown here winning his first race of the season, at the Belgian Grand Prix at Spa. He also won in Monaco and Italy to become the World Champion ahead of his team-mate, Gilles Villeneuve. The 1979 season did not go to plan since the all-conquering Lotus 79s of the previous year were left behind by the opposition and the French Ligier team won the opening races. When Lotus finally unveiled its Type 80, it proved too complex to develop correctly. When the Ligiers failed, the Ferrari's were there to collect the points. The year was also notable for the first World Championship victory for a 1.5-litre turbocharged car in Formula 1 during the modern era, when Jean-Pierre Jabouille's Renault won the French GP.

Opposite and inset: By the time of the British Grand Prix in 1979, the Williams FW07 had shown a dramatic improvement and the Australian driver Alan Jones took pole position at Silverstone, ahead of the Renault turbo of Jean-Pierre Jabouille that had won the previous race in France. At the start of the race, Jones led from Jabouille with the second Williams of Clay Regazzoni slotting into third ahead of the Brabham of Nelson Piquet. The Williams team had never won a Grand Prix and, with new Saudi-based sponsorship, it seemed that Jones would supply the first victory. Just after the half-way stage of the race, the engine overheated in Jones' car and he retired to leave Clay Regazzoni to take the win, ahead of the Renault of Rene Arnoux.

Right: Bernie Ecclestone purchased the Brabham team at the start of 1972 and in 1973 employed Gordon Murray as the designer. At the end of the 1970s, the team used Alfa Romeo engines but the older Ford Cosworth still had power and reliability. For the 1980 season, the team returned to the Cosworth DFV and Murray revised the BT49. This enabled Nelson Piquet, seen here at the South African Grand Prix, to score three wins during the year to take second place in the championship. The following year, another three wins and some consistent points finishes saw Piquet become the World Champion for 1981.

Left: The distinctive crash helmet of Canadian driver Gilles Villeneuve in the cockpit of his Ferrari at the South African Grand Prix, 1980. Villeneuve entered Formula 1 in 1977 in a McLaren and his natural speed impressed Enzo Ferrari; within a month, he was driving for the Italian team. Unfortunately, the Ferrari cars were not the most competitive at the time and 1978 was spent learning the business while 1979 saw him supporting the team leader Jody Scheckter. The Ferrari 312T5 of 1980 was almost undriveable and he could only accumulate six points during the whole season. In 1981, the V12 engine had enough power to haul the agricultural chassis to two race wins, while Villeneuve established his reputation for incredible car control and total determination to race, even on three wheels if necessary. His obvious ability and love of racing made him a folk hero amongst race fans around the world, more so than any other driver – it was only time before he became World Champion. In 1982, the Ferrari suffered reliability problems until the Imola Grand Prix in Italy. Villeneuve was coasting to the finish line when his team-mate, Didier Pironi, suddenly went past to grab victory, despite being instructed to maintain his position behind Villeneuve. The drivers had agreed amongst themselves to support each other and this betrayal incensed Villeneuve. He determined never to speak to Pironi again. Two weeks later, whilst practicing in Belgium, his Ferrari ran into the back of another competitor and Formula 1 lost one of its greatest talents.

Opposite: The Williams-Cosworth FW07s of Alan Jones and Carlos Reutemann at the British Grand Prix, 1980. The drivers finished first and third in the race and the Drivers Championship, split by the remarkably fast Brabham BT49 of Nelson Piquet.

Above: For 1981, Renault lured Alain Prost away from McLaren to drive its turbo cars alongside Rene Arnoux. The RE20 proved uncompetitive, but when the 560bhp RE30 arrived halfway through the season, Prost took three wins and two second places to finish fifth in the championship, just seven points behind the winner, Nelson Piquet. This proved to be the high point for the Renaults as the RE30 won just four races during 1982, shared between the two drivers; retirements spoiled a season which began in such promising fashion. Due to such a poor return on its investment, the Renault cars left Grand Prix racing in 1985 but the French maker continued to supply engines to Lotus in 1986. It returned as an engine supplier between 1988 and 1997 before a full return in 2002 when it purchased the Benetton team.

Opposite: In 1981, McLaren built the MP4/1, the first carbonfibre composite car and Irishman John Watson won the British Grand Prix with the car that year. Success proved elusive for McLaren throughout 1981, not helped by having Marlboro-sponsored driver Andrea de Cesaris in the team. Watson was a talented, intuitive driver who could, on his day, prove a match for anyone in Formula 1. 1981 was a turbulent time in the sport, with threats of a breakaway series being established and an uneasy truce formulated with a policy called the Concorde Agreement. Due to the unrest, tyre supplier Goodyear left the sport and was replaced by Avon and Pirelli.

Opposite: Niki Lauda returned to Grand Prix racing in 1982, following his earlier sudden retirement at the end of 1979. He is shown here winning the British Grand Prix at Brands Hatch in a McLaren MP4/1B, one of two victories he recorded that year. 1982 saw no fewer than 11 drivers share victory at the 15 Grand Prix races and one of the favourites to win the title that year was Ferrari's Didier Pironi. At Brands Hatch, he finished second to Lauda to take the lead in the championship, but a few weeks later, he suffered dreadful injuries in an accident that echoed that of the late Gilles Villeneuve just three months earlier. Practicing in wet conditions in Germany, Pironi ran into the back of Prost's Renault and took off; Pironi survived but his leg injuries meant he would never race again.

Right: Keke Rosberg took the World Championship for Williams in 1982, despite winning just one Grand Prix, although no driver won more than two races during the year. He joined the Williams team after Alan Jones retired at the end of 1981 and, when Carlos Reutemann walked out after two races, he became team leader. Keke was a revelation as he threw his car around with abandon and often went round corners using armfuls of opposite lock. His championship victory was notable since by now the turbo-engined cars were winning and the normally-aspirated Cosworth engine of the Williams suffered from a deficit of horsepower. The Brands Hatch circuit suited Rosberg's style and he put the Williams on pole before technical problems forced him to retire in the race. 1982 also saw the end of aluminium chassis as carbonfibre became the material of choice.

Opposite: Keke Rosberg's Williams in pursuit of Alain Prost's Renault, Monaco, 1983. Reigning World Champion Rosberg finished the 1983 season in fifth place but the highlight of his year was a victory at Monaco. The turbocharged Renaults and Ferraris were fastest in practice, with Rosberg flinging his Williams to fifth place on the grid. At the start of the race, Prost's Renault went into the lead on a wet track. Only the Williams drivers elected to use slick tyres and, as Rosberg immediately moved into second place, it was obvious that wet tyres were the wrong choice. Since driving precision counts for more than power at Monaco, Rosberg soon established a comfortable lead that he held until the chequered flag. At the end of 2005, his son Nico followed in his father's wheel tracks and signed to drive for the Williams team for 2006.

Right: The rear view of the 1983 Ferrari 126C3 that was unveiled at the British Grand Prix. Horsepower was in plentiful supply from the turbo engine and Rene Arnoux and Patrick Tambay took the first two places on the grid at Silverstone but Prost's Renault went on to take victory with Tambay's Ferrari in third place. Ferrari won the constructors title that year but the drivers championship continued to elude them, with Prost beating Arnoux to the title. During the year, the controversial aerodynamic side-skirts were banned (due to the cars becoming unstable and dangerous if they were damaged) and Grand Prix cars now raced with flat bottoms.

Left and above: One of the handful of drivers who reached the highest level of the sport who might be fairly described as a 'genius', Ayrton Senna da Silva was totally focussed and committed to winning at any cost. If he had a fault, it was not being able to accept that anyone else might be as good, or better, than him in a Formula 1 car. He was given the opportunity to enter Grand Prix racing in 1984 by the small British team, Toleman, but quickly signed another contract to drive for Lotus for 1985 despite the Toleman contract still being in force. Shown here at the Monaco Grand Prix, the flooded track allowed Senna the opportunity to demonstrate his skill in a car that qualified in 13th place. Many of the faster cars crashed while Prost maintained his lead in his McLaren and Senna picked off the Ferrari and Williams cars until, after 31 laps, he was rapidly closing on Prost. Suddenly, the chequered flag was waved several laps early, since the conditions were considered too dangerous. Prost was relieved, Senna was incandescent with rage and Stefan Bellof, in a Tyrrell, was disappointed since he was catching both drivers in his non-turbo car that had qualified at the back of the grid. In hindsight, ending the race early may have prevented a huge accident...

Left and below: In 1984, the McLaren MP4/2 cars had TAG-Porsche turbo power and two brilliant drivers in Alain Prost and Niki Lauda, who dominated the season. Between them they won six and five Grand Prix respectively, but it was the wily campaigner Lauda who took the title by the narrowest of margins – one half of one point. (This was due to the Monaco race being stopped early and the FIA decided to award only half points). These pictures show the McLaren at the British Grand Prix, where Lauda secured another win as Prost retired, and Niki Lauda in the pits at the following race in Germany, where he finished second to Alain Prost.

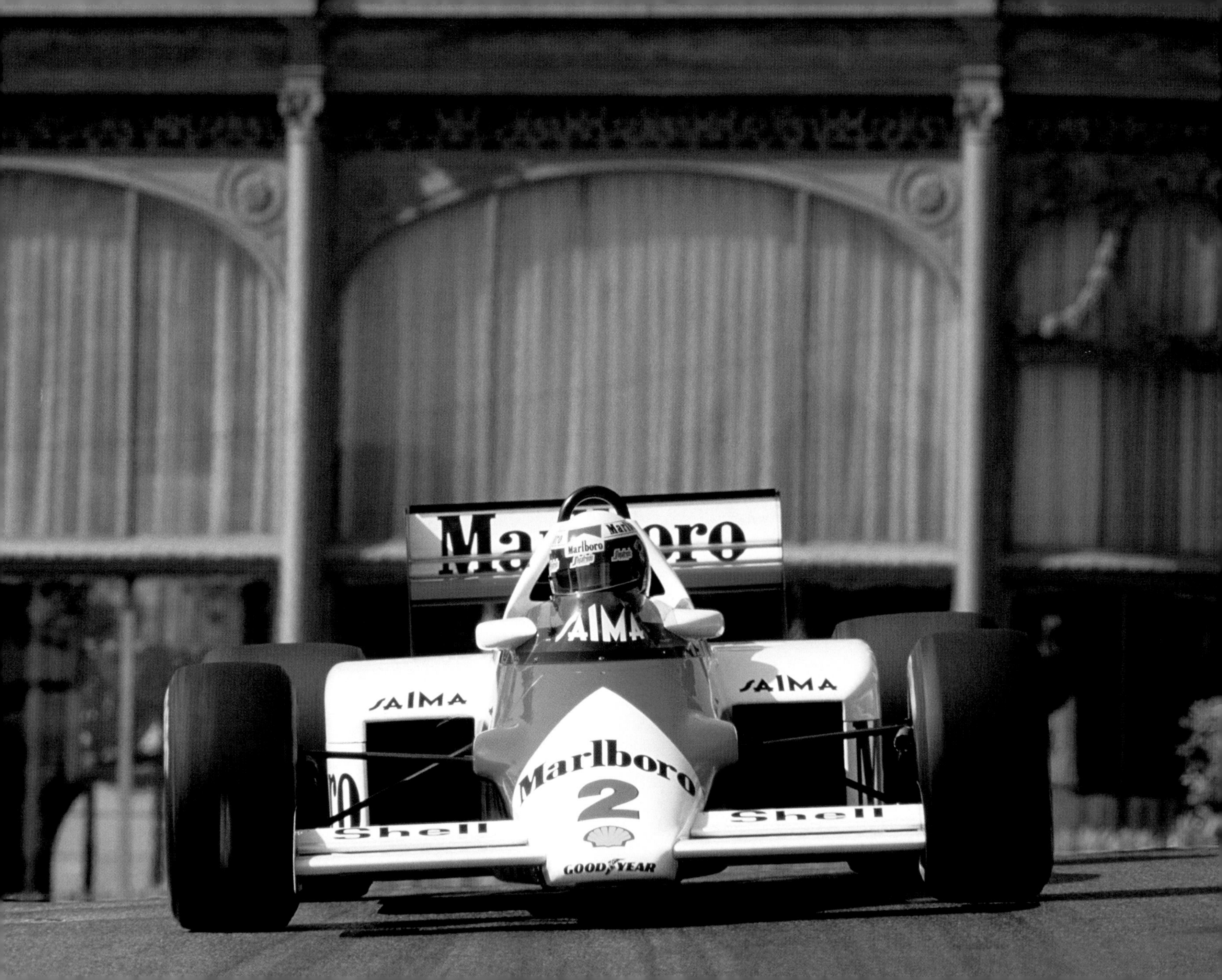
SAIMA
SAIMA
SAIMA
Marlboro
2
Shell
Shell
GOODYEAR

Opposite: Alain Prost in the McLaren-TAG-Porsche at the Monaco Grand Prix, 1985. Having lost the 1984 title by half a point, Prost was determined to put matters right in 1985. He won five Grand Prix, including Monaco, to take the title as Lauda suffered a season he would prefer to forget, winning just one race and retiring in 11 of the 16 races. He finally quit at the end of the year.

Above: Elio de Angelis was a prodigious talent (as well as a concert pianist of note) who arrived in Grand Prix racing in 1979 at the age of 20. He was signed by Lotus in 1980 and remained in the team until the end of 1985. He is shown here at the 1985 San Marino Grand Prix where he won, following the disqualification of Prost's McLaren for being underweight. He had no option but to leave Lotus at the end of the season when it was made clear that he would only play a supporting role in Ayrton Senna's challenge for the title. (Senna would not tolerate a team-mate who might challenge him; he also blocked the signing of Derek Warwick, forcing Lotus to accept Johnny Dumfries). Elio de Angelis moved to Brabham but lost his life during a test session at Paul Ricard in May. His unnecessary death resulted in new levels of safety at test sessions, since the correct level of medical care was not in place at the circuit, but it was too late for a driver who still had much to offer the sport.

Above: In 1986, the car to have was the Honda-powered Williams but nobody thought to tell Alain Prost who took his second World Championship at the wheel of a Porsche-powered McLaren MP4/2C. He was fast and consistent, winning four races to finish just two points ahead of the Williams of Nigel Mansell and three ahead of Nelson Piquet, the two Williams drivers losing the championship as they fought each other all year, each considering himself the number one driver in the team. Prost is shown here winning his first race of 1986, at the San Marino Grand Prix, where he finished ahead of the Williams of Piquet. For 1986, only turbo-powered cars were allowed, following the disqualification of the Tyrrell team during the previous season after it was found to be running its normally-aspirated cars underweight.

Left and above: The 1986 season got off to a bad start for the Williams team when its founder, Frank Williams, was seriously injured in a car crash following a pre-season test session. With the exception of the McLaren of Alain Prost, Williams-Honda was the most competitive of the 14 teams and Nigel Mansell, shown here at the British Grand Prix, came agonizingly close to winning the championship. He had begun his career with Lotus in 1981, but had little success until he joined Williams in 1985 and won the European Grand Prix at Brands Hatch. From then on, he was a different driver and silenced his many critics as his confidence grew. In a Grand Prix car, he feared no one, not even Ayrton Senna, and he drove with new-found speed and aggression. At the British Grand Prix, the two Williams cars lapped the entire field.

Left: 1988 was the year that belonged to the McLaren-Honda MP4/4. Ron Dennis took a calculated gamble and signed Ayrton Senna and Alain Prost to drive in the same team. Senna was desperate for a competitive car so had little choice but to accept Prost as his team-mate. Senna is shown at the Belgian Grand Prix where he recorded one of his eight victories, while Prost won seven. The team was denied a clean sweep of all Grand Prix during the year when a back-marker collided with Senna at the next race in Italy; Gerhard Berger inherited the win for Ferrari.

Right: Alain Prost is shown here driving to another Grand Prix victory in the McLaren MP4/4 at the 1988 Spanish Grand Prix as team-mate Ayrton Senna was slowed by electronic problems, finishing fourth. Just one week earlier, Prost had seen the darker side of Senna and realized that his team-mate was prepared to win no matter what the cost. At the Portugese Grand Prix, Prost had the faster car and moved to overtake Senna on the straight. To his amazement, Senna moved across as he was alongside and at 180mph, squeezed Prost into the pit wall. Prost decided not to back off and went on to win but he now knew that Senna had a different approach to racing. The FIA refused to take any action to defuse the situation with the inevitable result that matters deteriorated. At the end of 1988, Prost had accumulated more points than Senna but when the 'best' 11 results from the 16 races were calculated, Senna took the title.

Opposite: The Ferrari 640 of Nigel Mansell passes the Williams Renault of Riccardo Patrese at the Japanese Grand Prix, 1989. Mansell later retired while Patrese inherited second place behind the declared winner, Alessandro Nannini in a Benetton. The Japanese Grand Prix of 1989 was not Formula 1's finest hour. At the time, Alain Prost was leading the championship but Senna was catching him following a dominant victory in Spain. He had to win in Japan and Australia and qualified on pole in Japan. However, Prost took the lead and opened a small gap, but Senna responded and attempted an optimistic pass into the chicane. Prost either had to give way or hit Senna. He opted for the latter and the cars tangled. Prost left his stricken car but Senna demanded the marshals push him clear. He then jump-started the engine and drove off to win on the road. Afterwards he was disqualified for missing the chicane. McLaren appealed but the judgement was upheld and the FIA added a $100,000 fine and a suspended six month ban.

Above: For 1989 turbo engines were banned as Formula 1 adopted the 3.5-litre atmospheric engines. The McLaren team now used Honda V10 engines as Prost and Senna renewed hostilities. The FIA were desperate to break into the American market and moved the USA Grand Prix from Detroit to the streets of Phoenix, Arizona. Held on a bumpy track, with a sparse crowd, the race lacked atmosphere. Ayrton Senna qualified his McLaren on pole but retired with electrical gremlins. Alain Prost (seen here) went on to win from the Williams of Riccardo Patrese, although Senna had won the previous three grand Prix. In an acrimonious season, Prost went on to redress the balance from 1988 and won another World Championship.

Left: After the controversy of Japan, the final race of 1989 took place in Adelaide, Australia amidst an atmosphere of acrimony. Ayrton Senna and Alain Prost qualified first and second, but on race day, the rain poured down and for some time it looked likely that the Grand Prix would be cancelled. Eventually it was decided to race, despite the standing water on the track that would throw up clouds of spray and reduce visibility. With the World Championship settled in his favour, Prost (left) decided to withdraw at the end of the first lap while Senna (right) made the most of a clear track and opened a commanding lead. Several cars collided due to the spray and when Senna began to lap the slower cars, he could see nothing along the main straight and ran into the back of Martin Brundle's Brabham, destroying the front of his McLaren. Thierry Boutsen survived the conditions to win for Williams.

5 SENNA, SCHUMACHER AND THE APPLIANCE OF SCIENCE

(1990–2005)

As the new decade arrived, Formula 1 was in turmoil as the legislators tried to prevent technology from controlling the sport. New rules were introduced to reign in the increasingly creative interpretation of the rule book by ever more talented designers, in the vain hope that the cars would become more evenly matched and no one team would dominate. There was a genuine fear that the cars would soon become so sophisticated that they could almost be controlled from the pits with the drivers reduced to the task of steering. It was generally agreed that F1 had to remain at the cutting-edge of technological advance, but it appeared likely that the sport would be fought between designers with the largest budget, than between drivers.

Between the end of the 1989 season and the arrival of the first Grand Prix of 1990, the atmosphere within the sport was one of acrimony as Ayrton Senna refused to accept the decision of the FIA to exclude him from the Japanese Grand Prix and ultimately deny him the World Championship. He alluded to a 'French conspiracy' with the Paris-based FIA favouring a French driver. Such an outright attack on its authority and integrity could not continue and the FIA informed Senna that unless he accepted its decision and stopped his tirade, his F1 super-licence would not be renewed. For a while it seemed that he might not back down, but in the end, he arrived at the United States Grand Prix to resume what he did best – driving. His team-mate at McLaren was Gerhard Berger, who had exchanged his seat at Ferrari with Alain Prost.

Following the debacle at Suzuka, Prost received little support from his team and knew that it was no longer possible to continue with McLaren, so a deal was arranged that took him to Italy. Although Prost had made an effort to defuse the situation, it was to no avail since Senna knew he had to dominate any driver who represented a genuine threat.

Nigel Mansell remained with Ferrari, the only driver who had no doubt that he could get the better of both Senna and Prost. However, he had a fraught season and won just once as his two rivals established their authority and shared 11 victories between them. With two races left, Senna had established a small lead in the championship and knew that if neither he nor Prost finished the penultimate race in Japan, he would secure the title. Senna settled the issue in the most calculating manner by simply driving into the back of Prost's Ferrari in the first corner. Remarkably neither driver was hurt, nor were the 18 drivers who were following at racing speeds as the two collided, although several cars were damaged by wreckage that littered the track. After the problems of 1989, the FIA chose to ignore the situation to the long-term detriment of the sport. Senna was awarded the championship.

As 1991 arrived, so did a new Honda V10 engine for the successful McLaren MP4 that had so far won five manufacturers and three drivers titles. The engines could now rev to 15,000rpm and produced 780 horsepower and when Ayrton Senna won the first four races of the season, it seemed the McLaren domination would continue unabated. However, Williams had developed its Adrian Newey-designed FW14 with a Renault engine, a semi-automatic gearbox and traction control. Suddenly, the McLaren appeared to be vulnerable. Nigel Mansell had been signed as the undisputed number one driver at Williams, along with Riccardo Patrese and it was the Italian who first broke the McLaren/Senna stranglehold by winning in Mexico before Mansell responded with three successive victories. Senna came back with two further victories in Hungary and Belgium and, with points gathered from three second-place finishes, he took the title once more, 24 points ahead of Nigel Mansell.

That year saw the arrival of two young drivers who would soon challenge the existing champions; Mika Hakkinen joined Lotus and Michael Schumacher was drafted into the Jordan team for the Belgian Grand Prix at Spa where he qualified in seventh place. By the time of the next race in Italy, Schumacher had become a Benetton driver, a fact that was not greatly appreciated by the Jordan team since they were under the impression that a contract had been signed. Alain Prost suffered a frustrating year in a recalcitrant Ferrari and when he dared voice his opinion of the car, he was dismissed from the team prior to the final race of the season. With no time to find another drive for 1992, Prost decided it might be appropriate to take a one year sabbatical from the racing scene.

Had the Williams FW14 been a little more reliable from the beginning of 1991, it could have secured the title for Nigel Mansell, but for 1992, he put matters right and also created a new record when he won the first five Grand Prix of the year. A further four wins ensured he almost doubled the points tally of Riccardo Patrese to win the title by a huge margin. Even though the McLaren MP4 was no longer the best car, Ayrton Senna remained the best driver and continued to prove the point by winning three races, although he could only finish fourth in the championship behind the Benetton of Michael Schumacher.

Having secured the championship for 1992, the Williams team parted company with Mansell and promoted its test driver, Damon Hill (son of Graham Hill), to partner Alain Prost during 1993. Nigel Mansell had been involved in a series of arguments with the Williams team and, believing he was not receiving the support he was due, left to take part in IndyCar racing in America. Damon Hill did everything that was asked of him, backing up Prost's run to the title, as well as winning three Grand Prix in succession. Prost took the title with six victories. The sheer brilliance of Senna earned five victories in the latest McLaren MP4/8, that had reverted to Cosworth V8 power following Honda's departure.

Mercedes-Benz made its first tentative foray back into top level motor sport with an engine constructed for them by Ilmor Engineering and installed in a Sauber, following several successful seasons in sports car racing. The FIA experimented with a Safety Car, introduced to slow the field during races while marshals carried out their work in dangerous situations, while on the technical side, traction control and anti-lock brakes became essential. Tyre widths were reduced as were wings and spoilers while, to the despair of many purists, cars were now launched from the starting grid via computer-aided programmes that further decreased the input of the driver. To start the race, the driver simply floored the accelerator and computers took care of wheelspin and gear changes. Such technology was a step too far and the authorities banned it from 1994 in an attempt to return the control of the car to the driver and to try to make the racing more exciting for television. For the same reason, pit stops for wheel changes and mandatory refuelling were introduced, regardless of the safety issues and extra personnel need in the pit road. Away from the track, former World Champion James Hunt died at the age of 45 after becoming a successful Formula 1 television commentator who was never afraid to speak his mind.

Once again, in 1994, the Williams team parted company with the reigning World Champion when Frank Williams informed Alain Prost that he had signed the driver he wanted most – Ayrton Senna. Prost knew that his position would be seriously compromised and, after testing the new McLaren-Peugeot, opted to leave the sport after winning 51 Grand Prix. This, however, proved to be a pivotal year in Formula 1 racing and for many enthusiasts, the sport would never be quite the same again. The confrontation that everyone wanted to see was that between the established champion, Ayrton Senna and his major challenger, Michael Schumacher. It never materialized since Senna failed to finish the first two races; he spun in the first whilst chasing the remarkably fast-starting Benetton of Schumacher and in the second, while contesting the first corner with Schumacher, he hesitated slightly and was hit in the rear by Mika Hakkinen's McLaren. Senna then stayed out on the circuit, watching and listening for any sign of traction control on the Benetton since he was convinced that the car left the grid faster than any driver could react. The next event, the San Marino Grand Prix at Imola, was a weekend Formula 1 would prefer to forget.

The race meeting began badly when, during Friday practice, Rubens Barrichello was fortunate to survive a huge accident which left him in hospital. On the Saturday, Roland Ratzenberger, driving a Simtek, was killed, the first driver to die during a race weekend for 12 years. Ayrton Senna was deeply affected by both events and seriously contemplated boycotting the Grand Prix, almost as though he had a premonition of worse to come. He was persuaded to race but the trouble continued when a car stalled on the starting grid, another slammed into the back of it and debris was thrown high into the air, over the catch fencing and into the crowd where four spectators were injured. The pace car was deployed and held the cars for four laps before they were released and the race began. Senna lead from Schumacher but just two laps later, his car failed to turn into the flat-out Tamburello corner and slammed into a wall. Although the cars could now withstand such impacts, part of the front suspension broke away and entered the cockpit with fatal results. It was a freak accident and the almost unbelievable loss of Ayrton Senna reverberated throughout the sport.

The argument between the FIA and the teams continued as the FIA tried to control the increasing speeds while putting on a good show for the television cameras. The car designers rejected any impositions placed upon them as accusations of cheating and the use of electronic assistance continued. The jittery atmosphere within the sport was not improved when, just two weeks later at Monaco, the Sauber-Mercedes of Karl Wendlinger slammed sideways into the chicane barriers with such force that he was unable to compete for the rest of the season. The remaining races were contested between Schumacher, who was clearly the man in line to inherit Senna's crown, and Damon Hill, who was armed with the very effective Williams-Renault FW16. Unlike the Grand Prix of some 30 or 40 years ago, there was little respect shown between rivals as drivers struggled to establish supremacy. At the British Grand Prix, Hill took pole position from Schumacher by the narrowest of margins but on the warm-up lap, Schumacher went past Hill to lead the cars around, in clear contravention of

the rules. He was ordered to stop and serve a five-second penalty, which he chose to ignore. He was then shown the black flag, which he also ignored, with the result that Hill won and Schumacher was disqualified while the Benetton team complained bitterly about injustice. The Benetton cars enjoyed better reliability than Williams which enabled Schumacher to keep in touch with Hill, although controversy was never far away. At the German Grand Prix, the Benetton of Jos Verstappen exploded into flames in the pits when a fuel-hose nozzle remained open and fuel poured onto the hot engine. This was later found to be due to the team having removed part of the valve to allow a faster fuel-flow. The drivers now relied on faster pit stops to get past cars, effectively overtaking in the pits, rather than on the track. As the cars employed more effective aerodynamics, so drivers found it harder to follow the car in front prior to making an overtaking manoeuvre; they were driving in a form of vacuum that robbed the aerodynamic aids of air and downforce. It was not uncommon to see a car attempt to close up in a corner, only to run wide as the car lost the air pressure and became almost uncontrollable. It was claimed that a Formula 1 car began to be affected by this problem at a range of 100 metres, increasing in severity as it got closer to the car in front. At many fast, narrow circuits, overtaking was almost eliminated.

1994 ended on a suitably low note when the title was decided at the final Grand Prix in Australia. Schumacher led by one point from Damon Hill and the two cars qualified on the front row. The Benetton took the lead with Hill right behind and they held this formation for several laps before Schumacher began to pull away slightly. Maybe he relaxed or lost concentration, but his car ran wide and hit a wall, damaging the suspension. Hill had not seen this and came across the slow Benetton. Naturally, he tried to pass at the following corner but Schumacher had different ideas; his car ran into the Williams and broke a front track rod, putting Hill out and ensuring Schumacher took his first World Championship. It was a sad end to a sad year for the sport, since no championship deserves to be settled in such an unsatisfactory manner.

Following the tragic events at Imola and Monaco, the FIA introduced numerous changes to the cars, one of which was a reduction in engine size from 3.5 to 3 litres. Benetton switched from Ford to Renault engines and their greater reliability enabled Michael Schumacher to cruise to another nine Grand Prix victories to take the title from Hill. The season was extended to 17 races as Argentina rejoined the calendar just as the great Argentinean driver, Juan Manuel Fangio, died at the age of 84. The man who symbolized everything that was good about motor racing was gone.

In 1996, Ferrari succeeded in enticing Michael Schumacher away from Benetton with the promise of future glory (and some money) once he had helped develop its new V10 engine. The Williams team decided it needed a more competitive driver to accompany Damon Hill and signed the reigning IndyCar champion, Jacques Villeneuve, son of the greatly-missed Gilles, while cars were further improved with the addition of higher side cockpits and protection for driver's heads. It was inevitable that the Ferrari situation would not be rectified overnight and, while Schumacher grappled with the problem of resurrecting the Italian marque, the Williams drivers fought it out between them. In the past, IndyCar drivers had not fared well following the move into Formula 1 but Villeneuve had no such problem. He qualified on pole at the first Grand Prix in Australia and appeared to be on course for a debut victory until mechanical gremlins intervened and Hill went past to win. It only took until the fourth race, at the Nürburgring, before Villeneuve won in dominant fashion, although Hill was able to win seven races during the year to gain the title that his father had won in 1962 and 1968. However, the writing was on the wall since, during the year, Schumacher had hauled the uncompetitive Ferrari to three race victories. It was obviously just a matter of time before the team became a serious threat, a fact underlined by the sports supremo, Bernie Ecclestone, who went on record as saying that it was essential for the good of the sport that Ferrari win the title.

Instead of celebrating Damon Hill's victory, the Williams team continued its own peculiar tradition of dispensing with the services of its champion driver. The team had decided that Jacques Villeneuve was better suited to fighting off the challenge of Michael Schumacher and signed Heinz-Harold Frentzen to join him. Hill departed to the under-funded Arrows team, having proved his many critics wrong. Inevitably, any driver following in the footsteps of an illustrious and respected father will suffer criticism but Hill proved that he was as fast as anyone and even capable of taking on Michael Schumacher. Possibly his only 'failing' was that he lacked the ruthless streak to do what was now required. Even though he elected to drive in a non-competitive team during 1997, he came agonizingly close to winning when he overtook Schumacher's Ferrari in Hungary and pulled away to create a lead of 35 seconds before the hydraulic system failed. As his car slowed, Villeneuve was able to pass and win as Hill struggled home second, narrowly missing the Arrows team's first victory in its 299th Grand Prix.

A great deal of interest surrounded the return of Jackie Stewart who established his own team, Stewart Racing, in 1997. There was a notable absence of tobacco sponsorship on his cars and when Rubens Barrichello came home in second place at the Monaco Grand Prix, in only the fifth race for the team, great things were predicted. The first race of the 1997 season saw a McLaren victory for the first time in forty-nine races, since Ayrton Senna last took the chequered flag for the team. Normal service was quickly resumed as Michael Schumacher and Jacques Villeneuve traded wins to enter the final race in Jerez with Schumacher leading by just one point. Many pundits were concerned about the forthcoming race since the Williams cars were expected to do well at the circuit and few doubted that Schumacher would not hesitate to do whatever was needed to win the title, as Damon Hill had discovered. The Ferrari faithful were certain that the fight would be conducted in a gentlemanly fashion and that their driver would prevail. In the race, Schumacher took the lead but after the final pit stops, Villeneuve quickly caught the Ferrari and knew he only had to get past to win the championship. He caught Schumacher off-guard and pulled alongside into a corner where Schumacher blatantly drove into the side of the Williams but crucially missed the suspension. He hit the side-pod with some force but fortunately Villeneuve was able to continue on his way to the title. After the event, the official FIA stewards decided not to take any action against Schumacher, dismissing his efforts as a 'racing incident'. In the end, the best driver alive did far more damage to his reputation than any sanctions could, although later the FIA half-heartedly disqualified him from the 1997 championship.

Despite the reduction in engine size, the cars were now faster than ever. The FIA decided that the introduction of grooved, treaded tyres would prove an effective way to slow things down. Amid the usual arguments, claiming the cars would fly off the road, the teams assembled in Melbourne, Australia in March 1998 to start another season. To everyone's amazement, the two McLaren-Mercedes MP4/13 cars were uncatchable as they lapped the entire field, with Mika Hakkinen coming home ahead of David Coulthard. As expected, with new personnel and a truly huge budget, Schumacher was beginning to get to grips with the Ferrari, but it was Hakkinen who recorded eight victories to Schumacher's six, to lift the title and return McLaren to the top of the sport, with Coulthard finishing in third place. One race did supply an unusual result during the season when, at a rain-soaked Spa, a very unfortunate accident occurred between the Ferrari of Schumacher and the McLaren of Coulthard. Schumacher had earlier passed the Jordan of Damon Hill and quickly established a huge lead. The rain was creating huge clouds of spray and when Schumacher entered one, he slammed into the McLaren, ripping the front wheel off his car. Matters were not helped when Schumacher stormed into the McLaren pit hurling abuse at Coulthard and accusing him of deliberately driving slowly in an effort to cause an accident. The two Jordans of Hill and Ralf Schumacher survived the rain to come home first and second to give the Jordan team its best-ever result. Damon Hill was naturally delighted, even though he had been considering retirement for some time. He remained in the sport at the insistence of his main sponsors but finally left at the end of the year after a prolonged and difficult departure, a disillusioned shadow of the driver he had been a few years earlier.

In 1999, Ken Tyrrell finally gave up the unequal struggle and sold his team to British American Tobacco, which offered sufficient financial incentives to ensure that Jacques Villeneuve joined them to help develop the new BAR team. Other changes were taking place as Stewart negotiated an offer he could not refuse from Ford and sold his team. It was re-branded in 2000 as Jaguar Racing, amid much fanfare and publicity and, ultimately, failure. The slogan 'The Cat is Back' was sadly abused by journalists to read

'The Cat is at the Back'. The 1999 season promised to be a battle between the Ferrari and McLaren teams and it was Mika Hakkinen who secured three wins to two from Michael Schumacher before, at the half-way point of the season, Schumacher broke his leg during the British Grand Prix. The race was won by David Coulthard's McLaren, with the Ferrari of Eddie Irvine second. Irvine then won the next two races to challenge Hakkinen for the title and, with just two races left, the prize could have gone either way. However, Schumacher had returned and decided to help Irvine win the title for Ferrari. At the Malaysian Grand Prix, he made every effort to hold up the two McLaren drivers and succeeded, as Irvine won, Schumacher was second and a frustrated Hakkinen was third. At the post-race scrutineering, both Ferraris were declared illegal by the FIA-appointed scrutineers, which handed the title to Hakkinen. The officials at the FIA offices in Paris disagreed, declared the method of measuring the cars was wrong and reinstated the results. To guarantee the title, it fell to Hakkinen to settle the issue by winning the final race in Japan, which he did by leading from start to finish.

As the new century arrived, the battle for supremacy continued between the Ferrari and McLaren teams; Williams had fallen on hard times in 1999 with just one second place recorded by Ralf Schumacher while his team mate, Alex Zanardi, retired on 10 occasions and failed to record a single championship point. As a result, Williams looked around for new talent and signed Jenson Button, who was the subject of much criticism from the self-appointed experts who claimed he was too young and inexperienced. Yet he managed to score 17 points during 2000, while team leader R. Schumacher collected just 24; Button could drive but the BMW-powered Williams cars were off the pace.

During the year, it was Hakkinen who led with only four races left but then Michael Schumacher won all the remaining Grand Prix, collecting 40 points to Hakkinen's 15, to win his third title. More importantly, he had turned the fortunes of Ferrari around and brought it a 10th constructors title, the first since Jody Scheckter's victory in 1979. Schumacher had been rather put out by some rather uncomplimentary comments from Eddie Irvine during the year, so he was replaced by Rubens Barrichello, who was under no illusion that he was there purely to support Michael in all his efforts. Rubens would only be permitted to win if Michael was not in a position to do so and he was expected to move over to allow Michael to win whenever possible. His reward was the right to drive the second most competitive car in Formula 1, as the new era of total Ferrari dominance began. Naturally the team and its drivers were happy to accept the plaudits their success deserved, even though they enjoyed a truly massive annual budget, possibly more than twice that of any other competitor. Some of the lesser teams, such as Minardi, struggled with budgets considerably less than ten per cent of Ferrari's. Even so, Schumacher moulded the team to his liking and was able to extract the best from any car he drove. More importantly, he could not only drive a Formula 1 car faster than any of his contemporaries, but whilst doing so, he considered race tactics, analysed the information relayed to him from the pits and simply out-thought his rivals.

During 2001, Michael Schumacher collected a further nine Grand Prix victories to secure his fourth title. Williams signed the Colombian driver, Juan Pablo Montoya, from IndyCar racing and he was very happy to mix it with Schumacher on the track, although his driving style could be somewhat erratic. The year proved a disappointment for Mika Hakkinen who failed to reproduce the form of the previous season. He announced his intention to take a one-year sabbatical from the sport and his place was taken by another Finn, Kimi Raikkonen in 2002. He soon established his credentials within the team and McLaren decided that Hakkinen's services were no longer required. It was David Coulthard who finished second to Michael in the 2001 championship while the fortunes of the Williams team improved as Ralf Schumacher won three races to Montoya's one.

To rub salt into the wounds, in 2002 Michael Schumacher simply destroyed the opposition, winning 11 Grand Prix and appearing on the podium at every race, with Barrichello taking four victories to finish runner-up. Only Ralf Schumacher and David Coulthard broke the Ferrari clean sweep with one win apiece, as the Williams and McLaren teams fought over the remaining points. The 15-17 race victory domination by Ferrari compared to the 15-16 result established by McLaren in 1988, although

statistics tell only part of the story, since Juan Pablo Montoya flung his Williams around to secure seven pole positions, which were never translated into results in the race. During the races, the Ferraris were faster and more reliable, indicating that it was the opposition who were failing. It was also the year that saw Ferrari make the change to Bridgestone tyres as McLaren elected to stay with Michelin. This meant that Bridgestone had only one main team to supply and were able to match its tyres to the Ferrari chassis; by such decisions are championships won and lost.

The Ferrari domination caused a number of problems. Not least was the remarkable decline in television viewing figures that caused great concern amongst the higher echelons of the sport, since the value of the Formula 1 industry depended on reaching a huge captive audience. Spectator numbers also declined throughout the year as the Italian cars tightened their grip on the sport. Ferrari also suffered more than its fair share of negative publicity when team orders were brought to bear in the most unsubtle manner at the Austrian Grand Prix in 2002. Rubens Barrichello had been the fastest driver all weekend, started from pole position and led the race all the way to the final corner when he was forced to move aside to allow Schumacher to take the win and the extra four championship points. This was good for business but not so good for an alleged sporting event. The crowd erupted and roundly booed the drivers on the podium; Schumacher was embarrassed and tried to hand the trophy to an equally embarrassed Barrichello. Matters went from bad to worse when, later in the year, Schumacher almost got the sport thrown out of the USA when he decided to attempt a dead heat at the end of the race. He had lead the entire race but allowed Barrichello to close during the final lap. Rubens was somewhat confused when Schumacher slowed as he approached the finish line, forcing him to take avoiding action as he shot past to accidentally win the race. The cynical Indianapolis crowd were far from amused and made their feelings known. In the press conference, Schumacher claimed he had tried to stage a dead heat before changing his story to claim that he had tried to pay Rubens back for the lost victory in Austria. Whatever the truth of the matter, the resulting publicity might have sold newspapers but did little to enhance the reputation of

Formula 1. In the McLaren and Williams teams, drivers remained free to race under most circumstances and the FIA issued an edict banning such team tactics in the future.

The 2003 season was awaited with trepidation but to the relief and surprise of many, David Coulthard won the opening race in Australia for McLaren from Juan Pablo Montoya's Williams. Even more remarkable was the fact that seven drivers shared the 16 race victories throughout the year; at the penultimate Grand Prix of 2003, Schumacher, Montoya and Kimi Raikkonen all stood a chance of becoming World Champion. Michael Schumacher did what he can always do and came home first at Indianapolis, shadowed by Raikkonen (who was now consistently faster than David Coulthard) while Montoya said farewell to his chances with sixth place. Going into the final race in Japan, Raikkonen could only take the title if he won and Schumacher failed to score. Since it had been 38 races since Schumacher's last retirement, the odds were all on Michael securing a record sixth championship, to finally beat the record set by Fangio. However, Formula 1 can be a fickle business and the race turned out to be just that. Both drivers struggled in qualifying with Raikkonen eighth and Schumacher an almost unbelievable 14th on the grid. The McLaren was not working well but the young Finn did everything he could as, once again, a Ferrari spoiled his day. This time it was driven by Rubens Barrichello, who deprived Raikkonen of the points he desperately needed. Schumacher suffered a fraught race, struggling past cars to get into a points-paying position before suffering two collisions that dropped him back. He gradually recovered to secure one point at the finish in what was one of his least impressive performances. However, one way or another he had lifted his sixth title, while Raikkonen came so close he could almost touch the trophy.

In an effort to improve the television spectacle, the FIA introduced one-lap qualifying which was less than successful, although it did guarantee sponsors an equal share of television exposure. (In previous years, the slower teams such as Minardi, always went out to practice before the faster drivers took part, in order to ensure their sponsors logos appeared before the cameras.) Cars now had to enter parc ferme after practice and before the race, to ensure that they began the race in the same trim as in qualifying. Only essential safety work could be carried out under supervision. A remarkable side effect of this new regulation was a new level of reliability, proving that taking cars apart and rebuilding them before a race only created more problems that it solved. One of the reasons for the closer racing enjoyed throughout 2003 was the fact that, for one year at least, the rules remained largely unchanged, allowing teams to fine-tune their cars to make them more competitive. At the same time, Michelin significantly improved its dry-weather tyres, catching Bridgestone napping.

As the 2004 season opened, it was expected that Michael Schumacher would be facing a stronger challenge from several drivers, particularly Kimi Raikkonen, Juan Pablo Montoya, who had yet to really settle into Formula 1, Fernando Alonso at Renault and Mark Webber, who proved very fast on occasions with the ultimately disappointing Jaguar. In reality, 2004 divided the motor racing enthusiasts into two camps; those who admired the ruthless efficiency of the modern Ferrari winning-machine, or those who longed to see competitive motor racing, with overtaking, wheel to wheel racing and several drivers in with a chance of victory. For the first group, the year could not have been better as Michael Schumacher and Rubens Barrichello were in a different class, helped to a large extent by the Bridgestone tyres they alone had access to. The Japanese manufacturer had responded to the Michelin challenge and come back with the perfect tyre for what was, at the time, the perfect Ferrari chassis. For the second group of fans, who just enjoy watching motor racing, the season was an unmitigated disaster, due in no small part to the sheer lack of competitive cars from all the other teams and some very disappointing performances from the drivers. Michael Schumacher simply arrived at the appointed venue, drove to victory and repeated the performance as necessary. He won the first five Grand Prix, to equal the record established by Nigel Mansell, before being knocked out of the Monaco Grand Prix in a slightly bizarre accident while following the pace car. He had a habit of braking and accelerating with no regard for the car behind him, which had caught out drivers in the past, but this time he decided to do it in the Monaco tunnel. Montoya, flowing in close proximity, had nowhere to go, drove into the barrier but also made contact with the rear wheel of the Ferrari. The cheer from the press box could be heard around Monte Carlo, while the team management tried to get Montoya banned for 'deliberately' taking out Schumacher, since it ruined the 18 consecutive victories they had planned. In reality, the Ferrari was not the most effective car at Monaco and the eventual winner, Jarno Trulli in a Renault, would have beaten Schumacher. He was naturally somewhat irritated to lose his winning streak, so responded by winning the next seven races before Kimi Raikkonen managed to perform a small miracle with his McLaren, winning the Belgian Grand Prix and giving a glimmer of hope that Formula 1 might once again offer the paying public a show once more.

Throughout 2004, Barrichello kept to the letter of his contract and dutifully followed Michael home on seven occasions, before being allowed to secure two wins of his own once the championship had been secured. Juan Pablo Montoya took victory at the final race, but in reality, the other teams were left fighting for scraps. Only Jenson Button at BAR made any real impression and finished the year as the 'best of the rest'. McLaren could not get its cars to work until the latter half of the season and Raikkonen was left frustrated after retiring in the first three races. Whilst nobody could deny that Ferrari was the best team in Formula 1 by a considerable margin, it was heavily criticized in the media for its lack of passion that once symbolized the company. It was now a corporate entity that churned out race wins and champions as if they were white goods. The people that loved the sport now had genuine fears for its future.

For 2005, the season expanded to 19 races with Turkey becoming the latest country to construct a suitable venue as the Grand Prix circus expanded its operations around the world. Efforts continued to control the ever-improving technology and ever-expanding costs. To slow the cars, the size of the aerodynamic spoilers was reduced and engines now had to last for two Grand Prix before being touched. An early engine change resulted in the driver having to start from the back of the grid, which was a problem that seemed to affect Kimi Raikkonen more than anyone else. As everyone sat back to await another onslaught from Ferrari and Michael Schumacher, the opposite happened. Suddenly it was Renault that had developed its car more effectively over the winter and it was Giancarlo Fisichella who took the first win of the season, before Fernando Alonso strung three victories together. Raikkonen suffered with mechanical gremlins in his McLaren before he could respond and the two young pretenders to Schumacher's throne fought a season-long battle. Suddenly, the Ferrari had lost its edge, the Bridgestones were no longer working as they once did and Michelin had made further improvements to give the other teams a fighting chance. Schumacher was faced with a season without a single victory other than that gained at Indianapolis, where Formula 1 managed to orchestrate a huge public relations disaster. Due to the nature of the circuit, Michelin could not guarantee the quality of its product nor the safety of the drivers. After much political wrangling, the cars took to the grid and the Michelin-shod drivers had no option but to withdraw, leaving Ferrari, Jordan and Minardi to drive around. The American spectators, unaware of what was taking place, left in droves and demanded their money back; history will record that Schumacher won the 'race'. The American Grand Prix aside, the quality of the racing improved dramatically, although the aerodynamics of the cars still made overtaking a difficult and sometimes dangerous operation. It turned out to be a frustrating year for Kimi Raikkonen as in the end the calm, considered approach of Fernando Alonso, plus the total reliability of his Renault, took the title, making him the youngest driver to become World Champion.

As the remarkable world of Grand Prix racing enters its 100th year, it continues to evolve and fascinate. The small private teams, with the exception of Williams, have been sold to large companies and manufacturers, as BAR evolves into Honda and Sauber becomes BMW. The politics of the sport will continue to frustrate as everyone wants to establish superiority and no doubt the ultimate prizes will be won by those with the most money. Establishing a level playing field in such a complex sport is all but impossible. What is certain is the fact that race fans will continue to turn out, or tune in, to watch the ongoing drama that is Grand Prix racing but ultimately, when the lights go green, the arguments and distractions are forgotten as the drivers do what they love doing most – race.

Below: Jean Alesi established his reputation by contesting the lead of the 1990 USA Grand Prix with the near-invincible Ayrton Senna. His performance stunned the Grand Prix world when his uncompetitive Tyrrell overtook Senna's McLaren, although Senna ultimately went on to win and Alesi held on to second place. Ken Tyrrell's team never regained the heights reached during the 1970s, despite signing drivers such as Michele Alboreto and designer Harvey Postlethwaite. The 1989 Tyrrell 018 was a capable car but when the team accepted sponsorship from Camel, Marlboro-sponsored Alboreto had no choice but to leave. He was replaced by the young French-Sicilian, Jean Alesi. His precocious talent also netted a second place at Monaco before Ferrari stepped in to sign him to partner Alain Prost at Maranello. Tyrrell cars would never enjoy a top-two finish again and slipped to the back of the grid, before BAR purchased the team in 1997.

Above: The podium at the 1990 Brazilian Grand Prix, where Alain Prost (centre) achieved his first victory for Ferrari. He is flanked by Gerhard Berger, left, and Ayrton Senna, right. Prost knew that he would have to leave McLaren at the end of 1989, since his relationship with Ayrton Senna had reached an all-time low and Ferrari were happy to sign him. In Brazil, Senna looked set to win in his McLaren-Honda MP4/5 before a collision with a back-marker dropped him to third, behind Prost and the McLaren of Gerhard Berger. The podium was the one place where Senna and Prost had to be in close proximity. On the track, the two drivers dominated the season, winning all but three races, but sadly, the championship would be settled amidst further controversy.

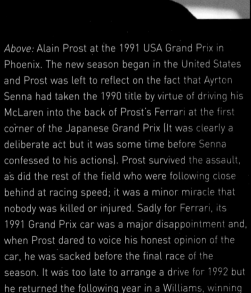

Above: Alain Prost at the 1991 USA Grand Prix in Phoenix. The new season began in the United States and Prost was left to reflect on the fact that Ayrton Senna had taken the 1990 title by virtue of driving his McLaren into the back of Prost's Ferrari at the first corner of the Japanese Grand Prix (It was clearly a deliberate act but it was some time before Senna confessed to his actions). Prost survived the assault, as did the rest of the field who were following close behind at racing speed; it was a minor miracle that nobody was killed or injured. Sadly for Ferrari, its 1991 Grand Prix car was a major disappointment and, when Prost dared to voice his honest opinion of the car, he was sacked before the final race of the season. It was too late to arrange a drive for 1992 but he returned the following year in a Williams, winning seven races to lift the title for the fourth time.

Above: In 1992, new drivers were emerging to challenge the 'old guard' of Prost and Senna. Mika Hakkinen joined Lotus, Michael Schumacher joined Jordan for one race before being 'acquired' by Benetton while the long-suffering Brabham team drafted Damon Hill into its Brabham-Judd for three races before the team finally left Grand Prix racing mid-season. Crippled by debt and chaotic managerial problems, Brabham began 1992 with Eric van de Poele and lady driver Giovanni Amati. When her sponsorship money failed to arrive, Williams test driver Damon Hill agreed to try to qualify the car. Shown here at his first Grand Prix in Spain, he failed to make the grid. He did qualify the car on two occasions but was lapped four times in each race. Brabham gave up the struggle while Hill went on to better things.

Above: Michael Schumacher at the Spanish Grand Prix, 1992, in the Benetton-Cosworth. Schumacher had risen through the ranks of Formula Ford and Formula 3 before showing his potential in the Sauber-Mercedes sports cars. He signed to drive for Benetton in controversial circumstances (Eddie Jordan was under the impression he had agreed to drive for his team) and instantly showed a remarkable blend of speed, tactical skill, natural car control and ruthless aggression that threatened to challenge the supremacy of Ayrton Senna. The world awaited the inevitable clash when the two drivers had equal cars, but in 1992, Nigel Mansell dominated the season in his Williams-Renault FW14B, winning the first five races. His team-mate, Riccardo Patrese, was second in the championship while Schumacher gave notice of intent with a strong third place ahead of Senna's McLaren, winning at Spa to secure the first of many Grand Prix victories.

Above: Ayrton Senna was a charismatic racing driver but a very complex person. His innate skill was beyond doubt although he probably spent more time than he should analysing every aspect of his ability. In this photograph, he is shown in conversation with the McLaren designer Adrian Newey (left) at Imola, 1994. He was seriously concerned about safety at the circuit following the death of Roland Ratzenberger during practice, to the extent that he considered withdrawing. After much deliberation, he decided to race and planned to fly the flag of Austria, in memory of Ratzenberger, after the Grand Prix. In the end, it never happened as Senna failed to negotiate the high-speed Tamburello corner and slammed into the barriers at 180mph. Grand Prix racing lost its greatest driver.

Left: Damon Hill proved to be a very competent test driver for the Williams team. He was awarded a place in the team for the 1993 season, where he partnered Alain Prost. Seen here at the British Grand Prix, 1993, Hill convinced anyone who doubted him that having a famous father does not guarantee a place in any team, it has to be earned. He won three races during the year, finishing third in the championship behind Alain Prost, before winning the title in 1996.

Above: During 1994, the McLaren-Peugeot and Ferrari Grand Prix cars were not the most competitive in the field and often qualified around the middle of the grid. At the 1994 European Grand Prix, held at the Jerez circuit, the early stages of the race saw the Ferrari 412T of Jean Alesi (left) trying to pass the McLaren-Peugeot MP4/9 of Martin Brundle (right). Alesi was famed for being a hard charger who was always late on the brakes, but here he clearly mis-timed his attack and almost collected the McLaren.

Opposite: The first corner at the Monaco Grand Prix is notoriously narrow. It is essential that the cars file through in sensible fashion at the start of the race, but in 1995, the Williams-Renault FW17 of David Coulthard was slow off the line and found itself in a Ferrari sandwich. Three abreast into Ste Devote corner will never work as Coulthard discovered when he tangled with the Ferrari of Gerhard Berger. The track was blocked and the race restarted; Coulthard dropped out with gearbox problems while Berger drove the spare Ferrari to third place. Michael Schumacher won for Benetton.

Below: Heinz-Harald Frentzen (seen here driving for Williams in 1997) was always going to struggle when he arrived in Formula 1 as he was referred to as the 'man who was faster than Michael Schumacher'. In 1989, Frentzen used to beat Schumacher in Formula 3 races and later, in Mercedes-powered Sauber sports cars. He made the mistake of moving to Formula 3000 in 1991 at a time when Schumacher made the transition to Formula 1. It was 1994 before Peter Sauber gave Frentzen the chance to prove his worth. His performances impressed the Williams team who made the decision in 1995 to sign him after Damon Hill's contract expired at the end of 1996. To everyone's embarrassment, Hill won the title but was immediately replaced by Frentzen. What should have been the perfect partnership proved to be a minor disaster as a clash of personalities saw the quiet German sidelined within the team, even though he could match his team-mate, Jacques Villeneuve, and won in Imola. Without the necessary support, he left Williams to join Jordan where he won two more races, but his promising career went into decline. He left Formula 1 in 2003 to take part in German saloon car racing.

Above: Mika Hakkinen in the McLaren-Mercedes MP4/11 at the San Marino Grand Prix, Imola, 1996. From the first time Hakkinen stepped into a Formula 1 Lotus in 1991, it was clear he possessed an exceptional talent, unlike the car he had been given. In 1993, he was signed to drive for McLaren, even though it already had two established drivers. When Michael Andretti decided to leave the team before the end of the year, Hakkinen took over his car and out-qualified Ayrton Senna in his first race. During 1993 and 1994, the McLaren team were forced to use Peugeot engines, which left Hakkinen struggling for results. The team acquired Mercedes engines for 1995 when his best result was a second place in the Japanese Grand Prix, but at the next race in Australia, he crashed heavily and sustained head injuries. He made a remarkable recovery and returned in 1996. Over the next two years he gathered a handful of points before, at the last race of the 1997 season, he finally won a Grand Prix. Although the result was a little contrived, it exorcized Hakkinen's demons and he went on the take the title in 1998 winning eight of the 16 races.

Above: The 1998 Ferrari F300 of Michael Schumacher leaving his pit. The 1998 drivers championship was fought out between the Ferraris of Schumacher and Eddie Irvine and the McLarens of Mika Hakkinen and David Coulthard. Hakkinen had finally broken his duck at the final race of 1997 and, with new-found confidence, he began to make winning a habit. Schumacher did not make life easy for him but with Hakkinen winning eight Grand Prix to Schumacher's six, it was the Finnish driver who prevailed.

Below: In 2000, the huge Japanese manufacturer, Toyota, decided to embark on an ambitious racing programme, to compete in both CART and Formula 1. The TF102 was unveiled to the press at the end of 2001 and arrived for the first Grand Prix of 2002 in Australia, driven by Alan McNish and Mika Salo. It was a promising debut, with Salo coming home in sixth place, a result he repeated just two races later in Brazil. During the next two seasons, the team scored a few fifth and sixth places as the cars threatened to become competitive but failed to live up to their early promise. It is a steep learning curve in Formula 1 and even the best teams have to run to catch up. A Toyota took pole position at the Japanese Grand Prix, 2005, but Ralf Schumacher contrived to snatch defeat from the jaws of victory – yet a Toyota will win a Grand Prix one day.

Above: Mika Hakkinen won his second successive drivers title in 1999, having fought off the challenge of Eddie Irvine's Ferrari after Michael Schumacher broke his leg halfway through the season. The title was only settled at the final Grand Prix of the year. No doubt Hakkinen was left regretting the races where points were dropped, such as here at the first race in Australia, where his McLaren-Mercedes MP4/14 retired with electronic problems.

Below: The Colombian driver, Juan Pablo Montoya arrived on the Grand Prix scene in a blaze of expectation. He had already won the 1998 F3000 championship and was immediately signed as a test driver by Frank Williams. When he lost out on a drive for 1999, he moved to the USA and won seven CART victories and the title in his first season. The following year he became the first rookie to win the Indy 500 for 34 years. His F1 chance arrived in 2001 when he replaced Jenson Button at Williams and immediately confirmed his reputation as a hard charger. He won four Grand Prix in his first season but the following year saw him unable to turn seven pole positions in victories. He joined McLaren for 2005 where he won one race compared to the seven gained by his team-mate, Kimi Raikkonen. Montoya remains one of the most exciting drivers in the sport, but has so far failed to do justice to his natural ability.

Above: Jacques Villeneuve with the 2001 BAR-Honda at Spa, Belgium. The BAR team arrived amidst much publicity in 1998, after purchasing the Tyrrell team, and promised to deliver a victory in its first season. BAR signed Villeneuve for a considerable sum of money but neither he nor the team engineers could make the car competitive. At first, the car ran with Supertech V10 engines before a deal was struck to use Honda engines from 2000. Success was still noticeable by its absence, so David Richards was employed in 2002 to revive the team and for 2003, the team drivers were Villeneuve and Jenson Button. Villeneuve was replaced at the end of the year by Takuma Sato and in 2004, BAR finished second in the championship, despite not winning a race. Having turned the team around, Richards was replaced for 2005 and the team slipped down the table as Button struggled while Sato threw the car into the scenery and, occasionally, Michael Schumacher.

Above: Jenson Button's BAR-Honda dives inside Giancarlo Fisichella's Renault into La Source, Spa, 2004. During the 2004 season, the Ferrari team totally dominated every race as the opposition seemed helpless to respond and a number of drivers appeared to lose motivation. One of the few who gave one hundred per cent throughout the year was Jenson Button, who finished the season as runner-up to the two Ferrari drivers, Schumacher and Barrichello. Jenson was signed to drive for the Williams team in 2000 at the age of 20. Frank Williams was heavily criticized for his decision, so Jenson responded in the best way possible, by demonstrating he could race as well as any established driver. Although he had several podium finishes during 2004, the first victory has proved a long time coming.

Above: Kimi Raikkonen in action with the 2003 McLaren-Mercedes MP4/18. The young Finn's arrival in the sport was not without some controversy since he only taken part in 23 car races in his life. Peter Sauber managed to obtain the necessary licence despite the concerns of many drivers. He finished seventh in his first Grand Prix and went on to score points in four other races to give Sauber its best season to date. It was only a matter of time before his remarkable skill and car control was recognized by a larger team and for 2002 he was signed to drive for McLaren. At the time, the McLaren MP4/17 was not the best car in the championship but he managed a second place in France. In 2003 he won his first Grand Prix in the second race and went on to finish second in the championship, just two points behind the all-conquering Ferrari of Michael Schumacher. In 2004, he was let down by an MP4/19 that retired more often than not in a cloud of smoke and 2005 started in a similar fashion, before the car began to work. He reeled off seven further victories, only to be beaten to the title by the more reliable Renault of Fernando Alonso.

Right: Fernando Alonso celebrated his seventh victory
of 2005 at the Chinese Grand Prix and became the
youngest driver to win the World Championship at the
age of 24. He had already become the youngest driver
to win a Grand Prix, in Hungary in 2003, and the
youngest to secure a pole position, in Malaysia.
Fernando began racing karts at the age of three and
progressed swiftly through the ranks until he was
signed by Flavio Briatore as a Benetton test driver in
2001. He was then 'loaned' to the struggling Minardi
team where his performances made everyone sit up
and take notice. It was no surprise when he replaced
Jenson Button for 2003 and made an immediate
impact in Formula 1. His lack of experience let him
down in 2004 when he tended to over-drive the car,
but for 2005 he displayed far greater maturity and
calmly went about his business to claim the title,
ahead of a frustrated Kimi Raikkonen. To everyone's
delight, he also seems to genuinely enjoy winning and
knows how to show it. It will be a huge surprise if his
2005 title is not the first of many.